Pat Summitt becomes head coach
of the University of Tennessee's
women's basketball team
1974

Bobby Orr wins his
eighth consecutive
Norris Trophy
1975

Reggie Jackson joins
the New York Yankees
1977

"The Thrilla
in Manila"
1975

"The Play,"
Cal vs. Stanford
1982

King vs. Riggs
1973

The ABA merges
with the NBA
1976

A GIFT FOR:

_____

FROM:

_____

Copyright © 2017 by Andrew Janik

All rights reserved. No portion of this book may be reproduced, stored in a retrieval system, or transmitted in any form or by any means—electronic, mechanical, photocopy, recording, scanning, or other—except for brief quotations in critical reviews or articles, without the prior written permission of the publisher.

This edition published in 2018 by Hallmark Gift Books, a division of Hallmark Cards, Inc., Kansas City, MO 64141 in arrangement with Clarkson Potter/Publishers, an imprint of the Crown Publishing Group, a division of Penguin Random House LLC.

Book and cover design by Ian Dingman
Illustrations by Andrew Janik

ISBN: 978-1-63059-696-5
1BOK1427

Made in China
0618

A HISTORY OF SPORT

An Illustrated Record of the Greatest Wins, Misses, and Matchups from the Games We Love

ANDREW JANIK

CLARKSON POTTER/PUBLISHERS
NEW YORK

OZA LINE STEVE YZERM
FISK "THE PLAY" BRAND
CASSIUS CLAY VS. SO
BARRY SANDERS PEGGY
LLING DOC ELLIS "THE
KERRI STRUG "THE BAT
OLAN RYAN SCOTT NOR
"THE RUMBLE IN THE J
ARD BOBBY KNIGHT RE
AMA" DIEGO MARADONA
MERICAN BASKETBALL
NADIA COMANECI WI
OMEN'S BASKETBA

PAUL W. BRYANT JO
CHASTAIN BOBBY ORR "
LISTON "THE BAD BOYS
EMING BILL BUCKNER J
AD STREET BULLIES" ST
E OF THE SEXES" RONNI
OD ARNOLD JACOB AU
GLE" JACQUES PLANTE
E JACKSON "THE THRIL
HE BIG RED MACHINE" T
OCIATION (ABA) "THE PI
A RUDOLPH FLORENCE G
HE FIFTH DOWN" 2001

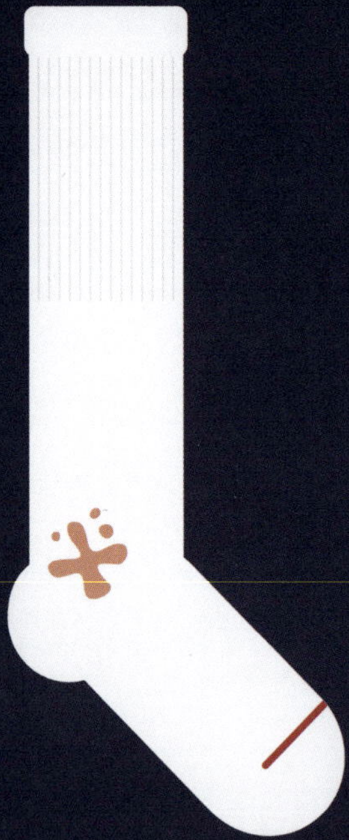

Major League Baseball
CURT SCHILLING
"The Bloody Sock"

Game 6 of the ALDS was also remembered for Alex Rodriguez of the Yankees slapping the ball out of Red Sox pitcher Bronson Arroyo's glove during an attempted tag by Arroyo.

—

Schilling would pitch Game 2 of the World Series on his still-injured ankle, again earning a win while his stitches tore and blood seeped through his sock.

—

The "second bloody sock" from his World Series start would eventually be sold for $92,613 at auction. The "original sock" was thrown away after Game 6 of the ALDS.

Curt Schilling, who began his career with the Philadelphia Phillies and Arizona Diamondbacks, was a key player in the Red Sox's 2004 bid to end their eighty-six-year World Series drought. After earning a playoff bid and sweeping the Angels in the American League Division Series, the Red Sox were matched up against their hated rivals, the New York Yankees, for the American League pennant. As any Yankee fan or Red Sox fan can tell you, things did not start well for Boston. They lost the first three games in the best-of-seven series. To advance they'd have to win four games in a row—something that had never happened in the postseason before. The Red Sox won the next two games, and Schilling was set to take the mound for Game 6. His ankle had been injured during the ALDS, and before his start, Schilling needed to have a tendon sewn back onto his ankle and stitched up in what became known as "the Schilling tendon procedure." Refusing to miss his start, Schilling took the mound. With his stitches tearing, blood seeped through Schilling's sock throughout the game. In obvious pain, he pitched seven strong innings, allowing the Red Sox to even up the series. The Sox would go on to defeat the Yankees in Game 7, capping an improbable comeback whose momentum carried them through to a World Series sweep of the St. Louis Cardinals.

> *It was blood, my blood, and it was coming from the sutures in my ankle. You're either stupid or bitter if you think otherwise.*
>
> —Curt Schilling

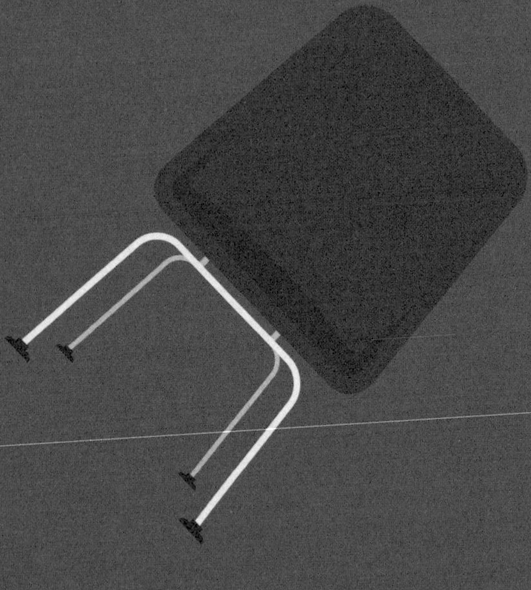

College Basketball

BOBBY KNIGHT
"The General"

Known for his intensity and temper, Bobby Knight coached the basketball team at Indiana University for nearly thirty seasons. Nicknamed "the General" for his demanding style and surly demeanor, he led the Hoosiers to three national championships, in 1976, 1981, and 1987. But Knight is perhaps best remembered for his outburst during a game versus Purdue at the Assembly Hall in Bloomington, Indiana, in 1986.

After a series of questionable calls against Indiana, Knight drew a technical foul in protest. While the opposing player from Purdue stepped to the foul line to take his free throws, Knight picked up a chair along the Indiana bench and threw it clear across the court in the direction of the referee who had drawn his ire. Stunned players, coaches, and fans looked on while Knight continued to berate the officials. Knight was ejected from the game. His tantrum stands as the iconic gold standard for over-the-top coaching outbursts.

At the time of his retirement, Knight had the highest win record of any men's college basketball team at 902.

-

The record is currently the second best, topped by his former player and assistant coach, Mike Krzyzewski of Duke University.

-

Knight's school coaching records:
Army (102-50), Indiana (659-242), and Texas Tech (138-82).

-

Hoosier NCAA championship wins under Knight:
1976 vs. Michigan
1981 vs. North Carolina
1987 vs. Syracuse

-

In September 2000, Knight was fired from the Hoosiers after a series of incidents prompted IU president Myles Brand to opt for a "zero tolerance" position regarding Knight's behavior. The night of his dismissal, Indiana students burned Brand in effigy.

> *Most people have the will to win; few have the will to prepare to win.*
> —Bobby Knight

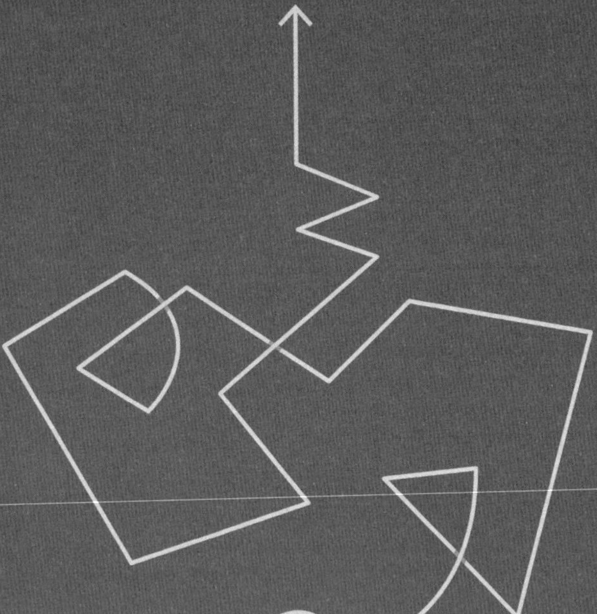

National Football League
BARRY SANDERS

In 1997, Sanders became the third player in history to rush for 2,000 or more yards in a season, finishing with 2,053 for the year.

—

Sanders's infamous touchdown "celebration" consisted of calmly handing the ball to the nearest official and jogging off the field.

—

While at Oklahoma State, Sanders played behind future Hall of Famer Thurman Thomas before taking over the starting role in his junior season.

After Barry Sanders won the Heisman Trophy at Oklahoma State University in 1988, the Detroit Lions selected him with the third pick in the 1989 NFL Draft. The Lions no doubt thought they were getting a great player, but what they got was a generational superstar. There has never been a running back with Sanders's abilities before, and there most likely never will be again. His agility, strength, speed, and elusiveness were unquestionably unique. Sanders made defenders look foolish, leaving them grasping at air with an assortment of jukes, spins, and cuts. He routinely turned negative plays into long gains, often leaving entire defenses in his wake. Peers, coaches, and fans alike marveled at what Sanders was able to achieve on the football field. After ten successful years as one of the top running backs in the game, Sanders, famously soft-spoken, abruptly retired on the eve of training camp for the 2000 season. It came as a shock to many, including the Lions. Sanders was just thirty-one, and many thought he had plenty of years of football left. The NFL suddenly and unexpectedly lost one of its most electrifying players ever.

We had a chance to get to the playoffs because we had Barry Sanders.

—Lions radio announcer Jim Brandstatter

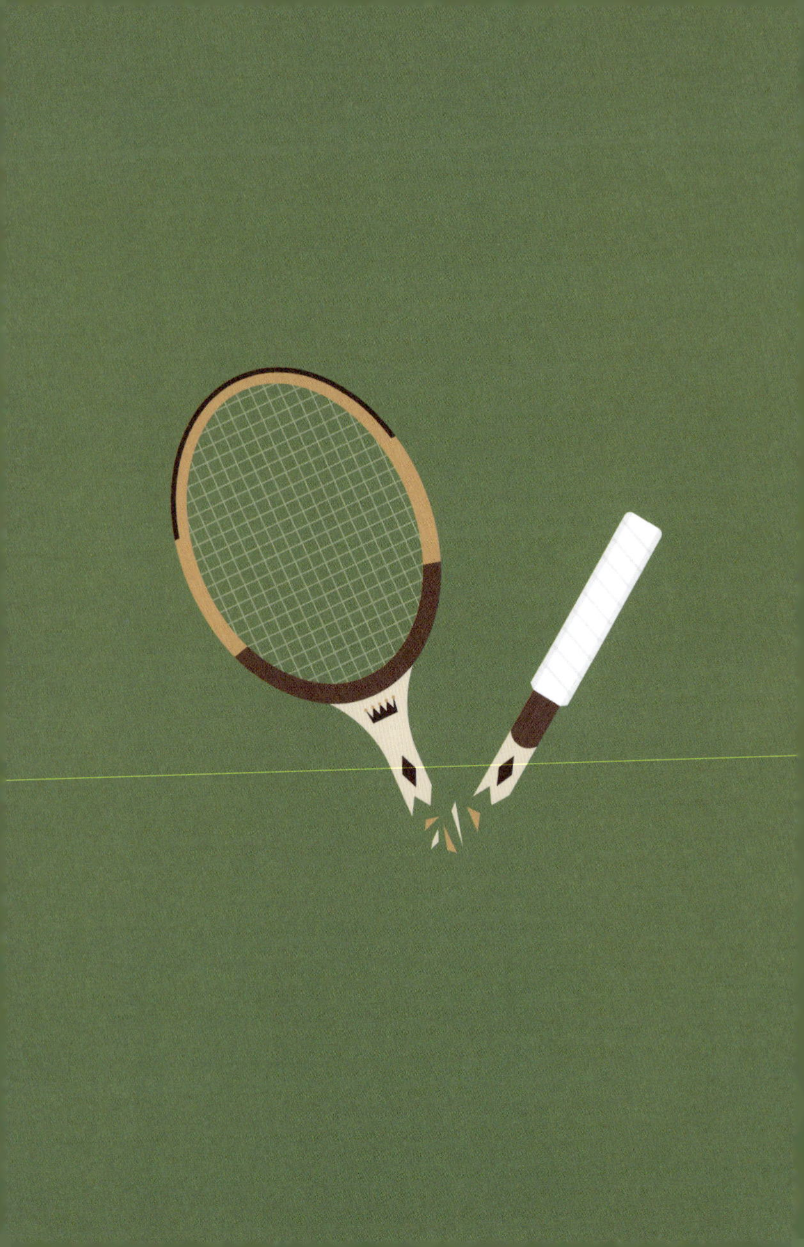

Tennis

JOHN MCENROE
"Superbrat"

McEnroe's most heated rivalry was with fellow American Jimmy Connors, as they faced each other numerous times over their careers.
It became so intense that both players needed to be restrained by officials during a match in 1982. This occurred during an exhibition match.

—

With 77 singles titles and 71 doubles titles, McEnroe holds the Open-era record for most overall career titles with 148.

—

In 1999, McEnroe was elected into the International Tennis Hall of Fame.

During the late 1970's and early 1980's, John McEnroe was one of the top tennis players in the world, winning seven Grand Slam titles throughout his career. His rivalries with fellow stars Jimmy Connors, Björn Borg, and Ivan Lendl helped popularize the modern game. As accomplished as he was as a player, his antics on the court sometimes garnered more attention than his play. McEnroe frequently clashed with officials and tennis authorities, often throwing and breaking his racket in mid-tantrum. He unceremoniously earned himself the nickname "Superbrat" for his wild outbursts, the most infamous of which happened during Wimbledon in 1981. In his first-round match against fellow American Tom Gullikson, McEnroe had a serve called out by umpire Edward James. As McEnroe pleaded his case to James, he became increasingly agitated, claiming his serve had drawn chalk and was clearly in. His tantrum culminated in his shouting at James the now-famous line, "You cannot be serious!" It remains one of the most famous lines in the history of tennis.

> *It's a fine line between genius and insanity in anybody who's the best at anything. John is the best player that's ever walked on a tennis court.*
>
> —former Wimbledon champion Pat Cash

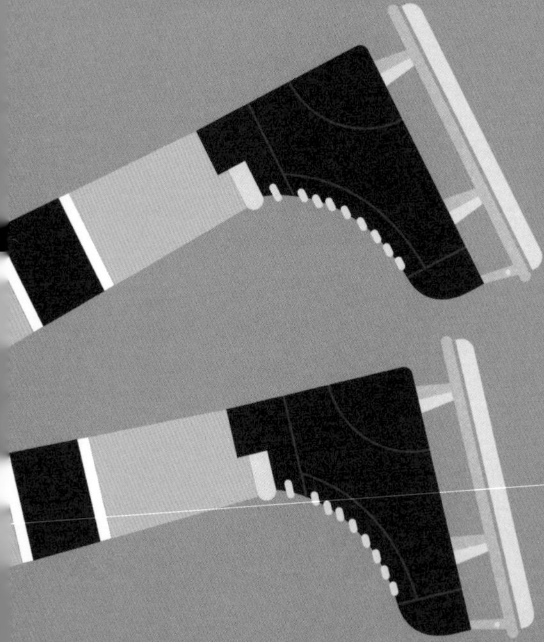

National Hockey League

BOBBY ORR
"Number Four"

Orr finished his career with 270 goals, ranking him seventh all-time among defensemen.

—

Orr won the Norris Trophy, awarded yearly to the NHL's best defenseman, in eight consecutive seasons, 1967–75.

—

In 1979, Orr was elected to the Hockey Hall of Fame at age thirty-one, at the time the youngest player ever to be so honored.

In his twelve seasons of tenacious, bruising play, Bobby Orr revolutionized the position of hockey defenseman, using his speed and skill (and often punishing his body) to realize the old maxim "the best offense is a good defense." Although he was considered small for an NHL player, Orr used his overt athleticism and fearlessness throughout his career to his advantage in the rink, becoming one of the most beloved players in the game's history. Orr's wild spirit was captured in an iconic Boston Globe photograph from the 1970 Stanley Cup Finals: With the Bruins leading 3 games to zero over the St. Louis Blues in the best-of-seven series, Game 4 went into overtime, the teams tied at three goals apiece. Taking a pass from the side of the net, Orr put in the winning goal, securing the Bruins' first Stanley Cup in nearly thirty years. In celebration, he jubilantly leaped into the air, soaring like Superman above the ice, limbs fully extended and parallel to the ground.

> *A defenseman, as interpreted by Orr, became both a defender and an aggressor, both a protector and a producer. Orr was more than an opportunist: he created opportunities.*
>
> —E. M. Swift, *Sports Illustrated*

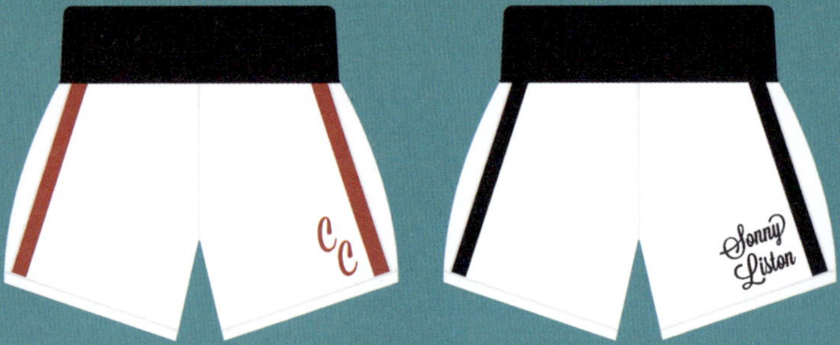
CC
Sonny Liston

Boxing

CASSIUS CLAY VS. SONNY LISTON

"Eat Your Words!"

> Clay's prefight taunting and all-out psychological warfare against Liston were a spectacle new to the sport, and a practice he would perfect and use throughout his career.
>
> —
>
> After the fight, Clay's camp would claim that Liston had tried to blind him by putting a foreign substance on his gloves. Clay essentially fought blind for much of the fourth round.

On February 25, 1964, twenty-two-year-old Cassius Clay fought the heavily favored and seemingly indestructible Sonny Liston for the Heavyweight Championship of the World in Miami, Florida. Liston was known in the boxing world as a force of nature, a powerful brute with a checkered history and ties to organized crime. At the time, Clay was known as a skilled fighter, having won an Olympic gold medal in 1960, but had been relatively unimpressive as a professional, known more for running his mouth than his boxing prowess. Not many gave him a chance against the veteran Liston, who had defeated former champion Floyd Patterson twice via first-round knockouts. Against the odds, Clay shocked the world, defeating Liston via technical knockout, as Liston refused to come out of his corner to start the seventh round, having been dominated in the previous six. Clay was crowned the new Heavyweight Champion of the World. Nine days later, he made an announcement that after joining the Nation of Islam, he would officially be changing his name to Muhammad Ali.

> *I'm gonna give him to the local zoo after I whup him.*
>
> —Cassius Clay

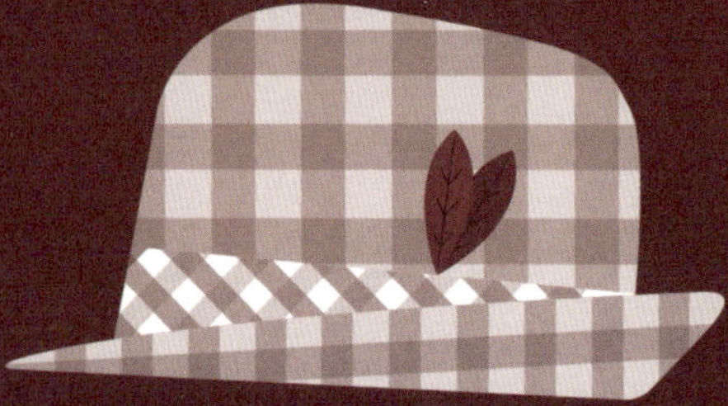

College Football

PAUL W. BRYANT
"Bear"

Bryant earned his nickname in 1927 by wrestling a muzzled bear at a traveling carnival.

-

At Texas A&M, Bryant put his players through a hellish training camp in the Junction, Texas, heat. At its conclusion, fewer than thirty "Junction boys" returned with him to College Station.

-

Bryant was so popular, he received one and a half votes for the presidential nomination at the 1968 Democratic National Convention (Hubert Humphrey would win the nomination with nearly 1,800).

College football has seen its share of legendary coaches over the years, but perhaps none is more iconic than Paul W. "Bear" Bryant. After beginning his career with successful coaching stints at Maryland, Kentucky, and Texas A&M, Bryant was hired as head coach of his alma mater, the University of Alabama, in 1958. He inherited a program that had fallen on hard times, struggling to stay competitive in the vaunted Southeastern Conference. Having developed a reputation as a no-nonsense coach, Bryant turned Alabama into a perennial powerhouse. Stalking the sidelines is his signature houndstooth hat, he shaped the program in his own image, focusing on aggressiveness and toughness, a formula that produced great results on the field. During his twenty-five-year reign at Alabama, Bryant would lead the Crimson Tide to 6 national championships and 13 SEC titles. He retired in 1982 having never finished a season with a losing record. A football man to the end, Bryant would pass away less than a month after coaching his final game. He remains one of the most successful college football coaches in history.

> *I'll put you through hell, but at the end of it all we'll be champions.*
>
> —Paul W. "Bear" Bryant

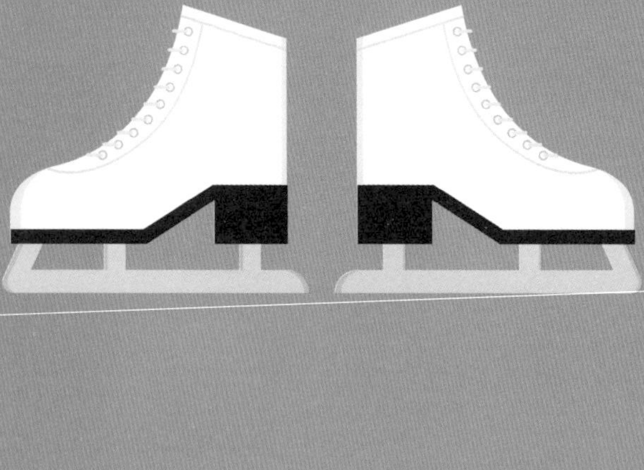

Fleming's mother made the iconic green dress she wore during her Olympic triumph.

—

In 1974, Fleming was elected to the US Olympic Hall of Fame.

—

Fleming has been a skating commentator since the early 1980s.

Olympic Figure Skating
PEGGY FLEMING
"The Original Ice Princess"

During the early 1960's, figure skating in the United States was facing an uncertain future. Tragedy had struck in 1961 when a plane carrying the entire US team and coaching staff crashed outside Brussels, Belgium, killing everyone on board. The shocking loss created an uneasy feeling toward the sport, one the United States had previously dominated. As interest in the sport waned, its return to prominence was sparked by Peggy Fleming, a young skater from California. Elegant and smooth on the ice, Fleming won the first of her five consecutive US championships in 1964 at the age of fifteen. Her greatest achievement came at the 1968 Winter Olympics in Grenoble, France, where she won the gold medal in women's figure skating, the only gold the United States would win at that year's games. Fleming's ascent marked a return to the top of the skating world for the United States.

> *The first thing is to love your sport. Never do it to please someone else. It has to be yours.*
> —Peggy Fleming

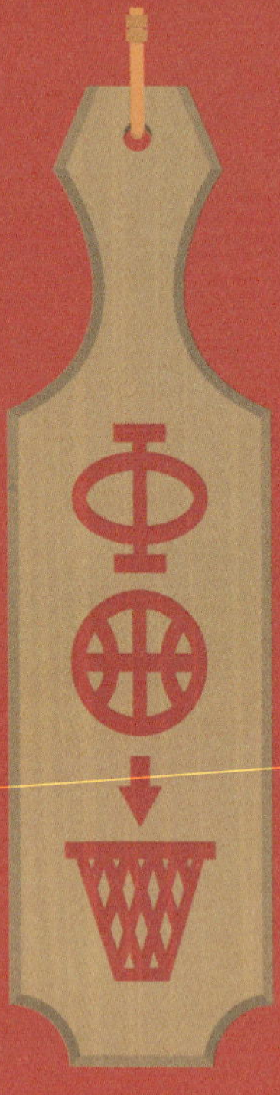

College Basketball

"PHI SLAMA JAMA"

University of Houston Cougars, 1982–84

For the men of "Phi Slama Jama," as this University of Houston hoops squad was known, the strategy was all about the fast break and the dunk, their breakneck pace standing in stark contrast to their opponents' slower, fundamentals-focused approach. The results were clear. With a roster including future NBA Hall of Famers Hakeem Olajuwon and Clyde Drexler, coach Guy Lewis led the Cougars to three straight Final Four appearances, advancing to the championship game in 1983 and 1984. They would lose both years (ironically, they were defeated on a last-second dunk in the 1984 contest versus North Carolina State)—and they are often thought of as "the greatest team that never won."

Many consider the loss in the 1984 championship game to North Carolina State the greatest upset in the history of college basketball.

–

As a youth in his native Nigeria, Olajuwon excelled in soccer, eventually transferring the techniques he used as a goalkeeper to the sport of basketball.

–

The dunk was actually banned from college basketball in 1967, mainly because of the dominance of center Lew Alcindor (later known as Kareem Abdul-Jabbar) of the University of Los Angeles, California. It was reinstated before the 1976–77 season.

> *When you were under the basket, and they came down with all those thunderous dunks, you looked around for a bomb shelter.*
>
> —referee Hank Nichols

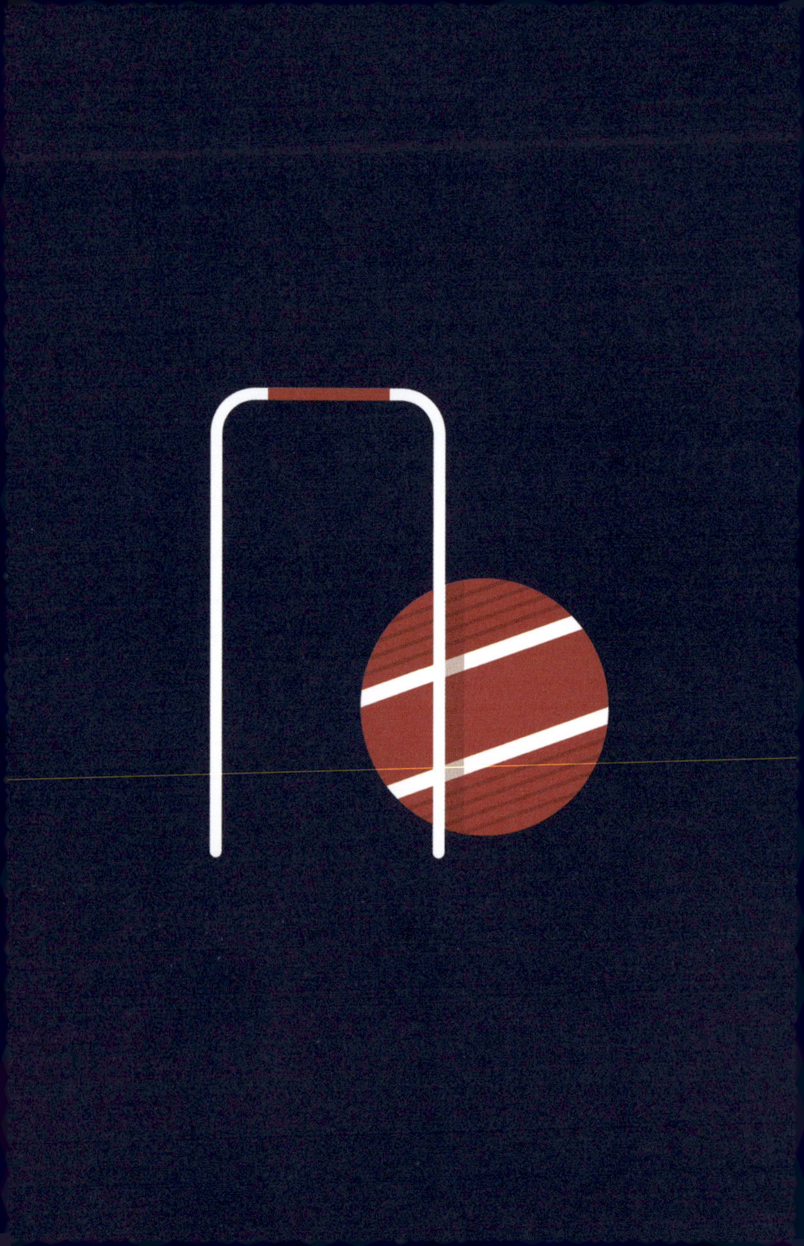

Major League Baseball

BILL BUCKNER
"Through the Wickets"

Buckner shouldered much of the blame for the Red Sox losing the Series, and he became a scapegoat for Boston fans and media. That contributed to Buckner's release from the team in 1987.

—

Buckner and Boston would eventually make amends. In 2008 Buckner was invited to Fenway Park to throw out the first pitch on Opening Day. He received a standing ovation from the sellout crowd.

—

In 2012 the ball that went through Buckner's legs sold at auction for $418,250.

Bill Buckner had a great career in Major League Baseball. He played first base for 5 teams over 22 seasons, compiling a lifetime batting average of .289 and amassing more than 2,700 hits. Those are very solid numbers by any measure. However, Buckner will forever be remembered for one of the most infamous errors in the history of baseball. It was during the 1986 World Series, while he was playing for the Boston Red Sox. Leading the favored Mets 3 games to 2 in the best-of-seven series, Boston was looking to end its long-standing World Series drought as it took the field in Game 6. The game was a tight contest throughout, with the teams tied at 3 after nine innings. Boston was able to score two runs in the top of the tenth, taking a 5–3 lead. But the Mets fought back in the bottom of the frame, scoring a run on three straight singles, all with two outs. Mookie Wilson stepped to the plate for the Mets, trying to keep their rally alive, but hit a weak ground ball toward Buckner at first base, which would seemingly end the game (announcer Vin Scully called the hit "a little roller up along first"). But the ground ball somehow made its way through Buckner's legs and into right field, allowing the tying and winning runs to score, and tying the series. The Mets would go on to win Game 7 and take the Series.

> *The punishment didn't fit the crime.*
> —Bill Buckner

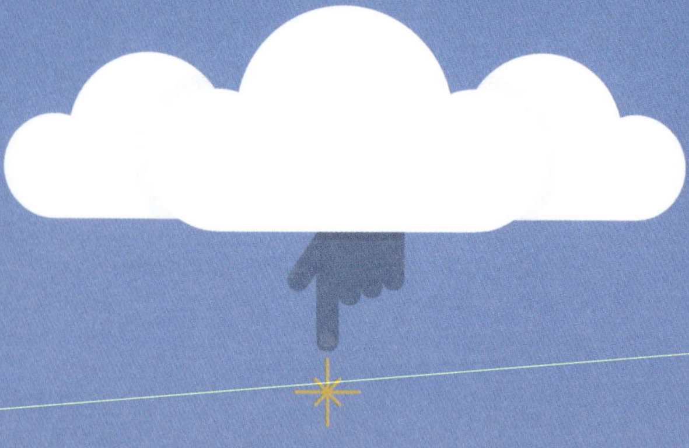

Soccer

DIEGO MARADONA
"The Hand of God"

Maradona was nicknamed El Pibe de Oro ("the Golden Boy").

—

Along with Pelé, Maradona was named the Joint FIFA Player of the 20th Century.

—

Maradona started in 21 consecutive matches for Argentina in four World Cups (1982, 1986, 1990, and 1994), scoring 8 goals and providing 8 assists.

Argentinian Diego Maradona took the soccer world by storm in the 1980's as one of the most dynamic players the sport had ever seen. Renowned for his vision and creativity, he was a force to be reckoned with on the field. Captained by Maradona, the Argentinian national team met England in the 1986 World Cup Quarterfinal. Minutes into the second half, a failed attempt by England to clear the ball from its own end allowed Maradona to seemingly head in the first goal of the game, over English goalkeeper Peter Shilton. However, replays clearly showed that he had hit the ball with his fist and not his head. Furious protests by England to the officials fell on deaf ears, and the goal was allowed to stand. It would come to be known as "the Hand of God" and remains one of the most controversial plays in the history of the World Cup. With the aid of another Maradona goal, Argentina would take the match 2–1, en route to winning the 1986 World Cup.

> *Diego was capable of things no one else could match. The things I could do with a football, he could do with an orange.*
>
> —French midfielder Michel Platini

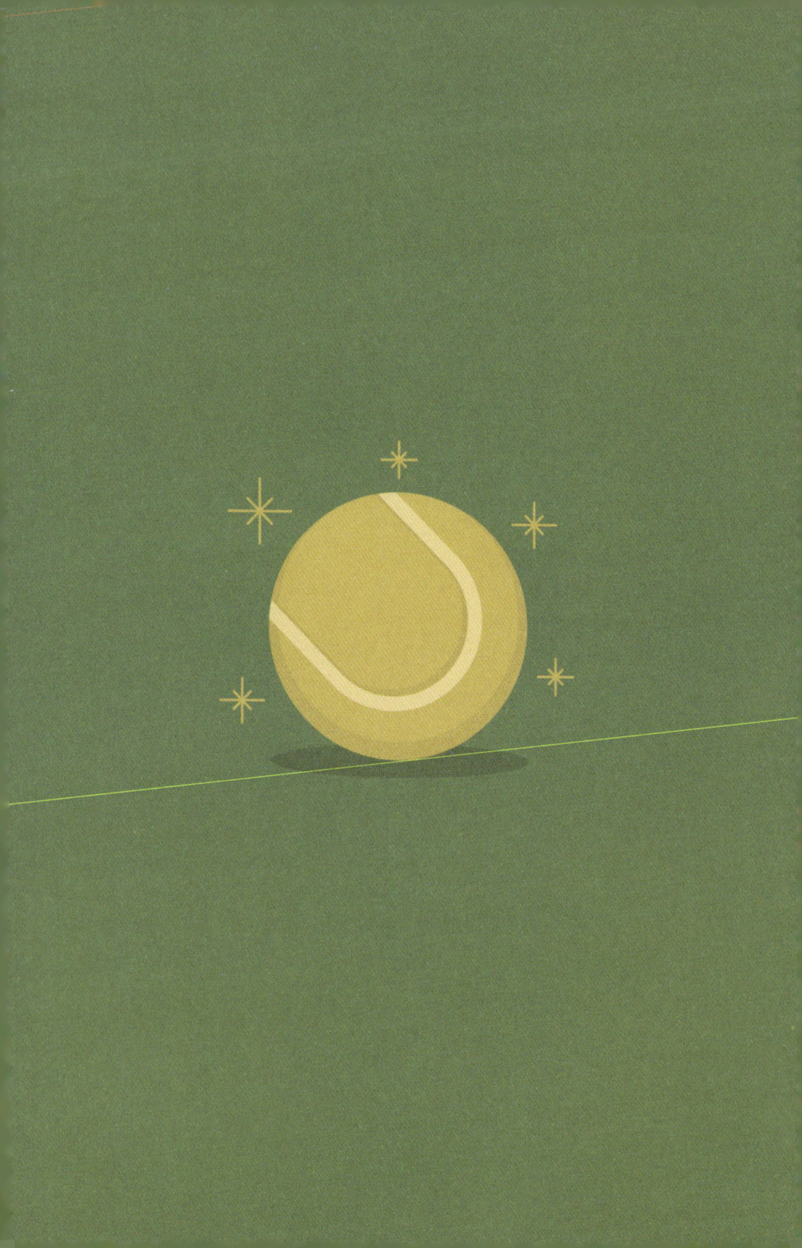

Tennis

STEFFI GRAF
"Fräulein Forehand"

Graf followed her Golden Slam year by being nearly as dominant the next, winning three of four majors, finishing the year with an overall singles record of 86-2.

–

During her career, Graf was number one in the WTA rankings an astounding 377 total weeks, nearly seven and a half years. Martina Navratilova ranks second at 332 weeks.

–

In 2001, Graf married men's tennis star Andre Agassi.

With 22 Grand Slam titles, Steffi Graf holds the record for most wins since the introduction of the Open era in 1968. Methodical, powerful, and precise, Graf amassed more than 100 singles titles and won an astounding 88 percent of her matches throughout her career. She also spent a record 186 consecutive weeks ranked the number one women's player in the world by the Women's Tennis Association (WTA), a tribute to her consistency. What sets Graf further apart from the other great players in history was what she was able to accomplish in 1988. By winning all four Grand Slam titles and an Olympic gold medal in the same year, she became the first player, male or female, to win the coveted "Golden Slam." Graf defeated Chris Evert at the Australian Open, Natasha Zvereva at the French Open, Martina Navratilova at Wimbledon, and Gabriela Sabatini at both the US Open and the Olympic Games in Seoul, South Korea. It is still a feat that no other tennis player has duplicated.

> *I never look back, I look forward.*
> —Steffi Graf

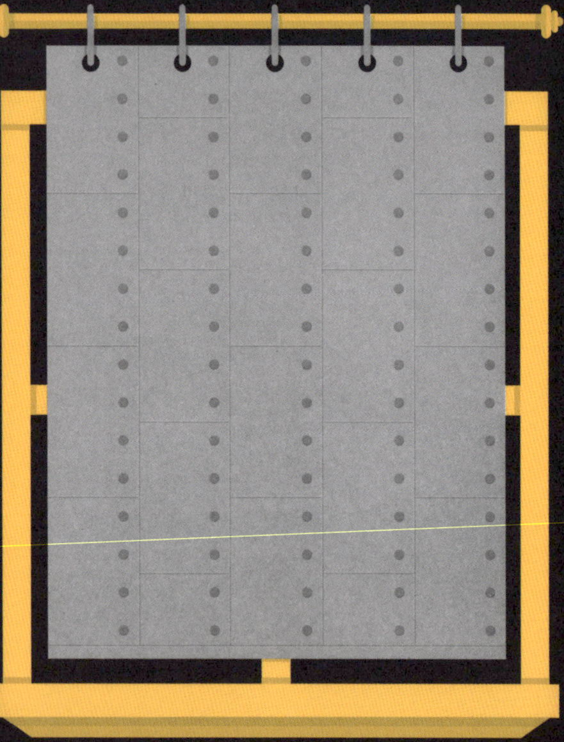

National Football League

THE STEEL CURTAIN
"Half a Ton of Trouble"

The Pittsburgh Steelers of the 1970's were one of the greatest dynasties football has ever seen; they won four Super Bowls over six years. Their success was in no small part due to their dominant defensive line. Including Hall of Famer "Mean Joe" Greene, L. C. Greenwood, Ernie Holmes, and Dwight White, they were given the nickname "the Steel Curtain" by a local Pittsburgh radio station. Large, physical, and intimidating, they wreaked havoc upon opposing offenses. Their brilliance was at the forefront during the tumultuous 1976 season. The Steelers were written off after losing starting quarterback Terry Bradshaw to injury. Anchored, however, by the Steel Curtain, their defense allowed only one touchdown over the next nine games, giving up an average of just over 3 points and propelling the team into the playoffs. Although they lost to the Oakland Raiders in the AFC Championship, their performance under pressure cemented their legacy.

The nickname was a take on the term "Iron Curtain," which was used by British prime minister Winston Churchill to describe the division of European nations after World War II.

–

During their 1976 campaign, the Steelers' defense allowed 50 fewer points than any other team during the regular season, giving up an average of only 3.8 yards per play.

> *Some coaches pray for wisdom. I pray for 260-pound tackles. They'll give me plenty of wisdom.*
>
> —Steelers head coach Chuck Knoll

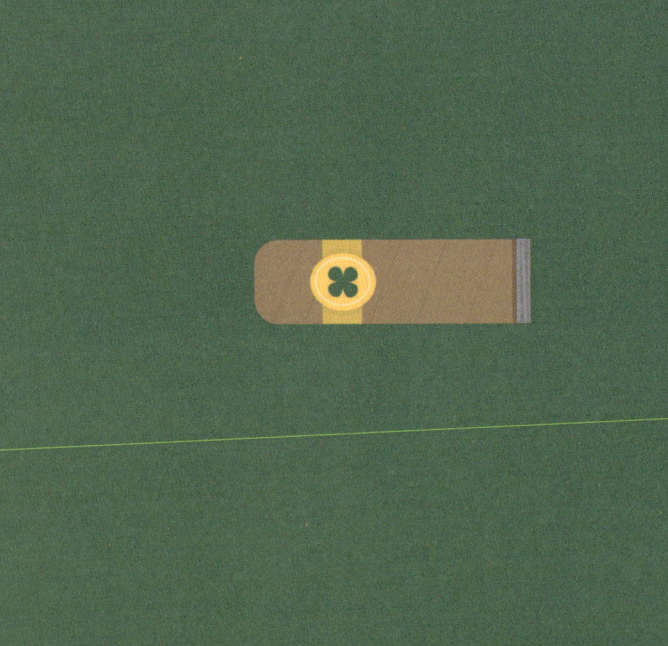

National Basketball Association

ARNOLD JACOB AUERBACH
"Red"

Upon retiring, Auerbach named Bill Russell his successor, making him the first African American coach in NBA history.

—

Auerbach was nearly as successful as an executive, the architect of seven Celtics titles from 1968 to 1986.

—

Auerbach is largely credited with the invention of the "sixth man," a starting-quality player who can come off the bench to spell a tired starter.

What Tom Landry is to football and Branch Rickey is to baseball, Red Auerbach is to basketball. As a coach and general manager of the Boston Celtics, he was part of sixteen championships in a career spanning almost forty years. He began coaching the Celtics in 1950, and his techniques helped change the way basketball was played, modernizing the sport by focusing on team play and the fast break. Auerbach also helped break down the color barrier in the game; he was the first coach to draft African American players into the NBA, including Bill Russell, who would go on to be one of the greatest players of all time. Auerbach coached the Celtics to eight straight championships in the 1960's, considered by many to be the greatest dynasty in the history of basketball. Always one to toast successes, Auerbach was frequently seen smoking his "victory cigar" on the bench when a game had been decided in favor of the Celtics.

> *The commissioner said you can't smoke the cigars on the bench. But there were guys smoking cigarettes on the bench. I said, "What is this, an airplane—you can smoke cigarettes but not cigars?" No way. I wouldn't do it.*
>
> —Red Auerbach

Olympic Track and Field
FLORENCE GRIFFITH JOYNER
"Flo Jo"

Florence married Olympic track star Al Joyner in 1987, making her a sister-in-law of fellow Olympian Jackie Joyner-Kersee.

—

Joyner would retire at age twenty-nine, pursuing ventures outside the world of track and field, including designing uniforms for the Indiana Pacers.

—

Joyner attempted a comeback in 1996 training for the Olympics but was derailed by injury.

Few in the sport of track and field had more style than Florence Griffith Joyner. With her custom tracksuits, flowing hair, and long painted fingernails, she brought a unique look to the sport. And she also brought something else: world-class speed. After failing to make the 1980 Olympic team and taking a silver medal in the 200 meters at the 1984 Games in Los Angeles, "Flo Jo" arrived at the 1988 Seoul games as a below-the-radar underdog. But in an incredible display, Joyner would go on to win gold in the 100-meter and 200-meter sprint and the 4×100 relay, as well as take silver in the 4×200 relay. In the 200-meter event, she broke the world record in the semifinal race, then broke her own record in the final, running the race in 21.34 seconds. Her performance was so stunning, it was met with a cloud of suspicion. Accusations flew that Joyner had used performance-enhancing drugs, though she did not fail any of the drug tests administered during or after the 1988 Games. Her 200-meter mark still stands, with no runner coming within .30 second of breaking it.

> *Conventional is not for me. I like things that are uniquely Flo. I like being different.*
> —Florence Griffith Joyner

C

National Hockey League

STEVE YZERMAN
"The Captain"

Yzerman holds numerous Red Wing team records, including most career assists, most goals scored in a season, most points in a season, and most career game-winning goals.

—

He is one of just 18 players to score 600 goals in a career, finishing with 692, two more than Penguin great Mario Lemieux.

—

Perhaps his most famous goal came in 1996, a slapshot from beyond the blue line in double overtime to beat the St. Louis Blues in Game 7 of the Eastern Conference Semifinals.

The Detroit Red Wings selected Steve Yzerman with the fourth overall pick in the 1983 NHL Draft. He headed to a team whose glory days were nearly thirty years behind them. Yzerman became the revitalizing force for the Red Wings, and by 1986—at only twenty-one years of age—he was named team captain (the youngest ever in franchise history). Over the decade, Yzerman turned the Red Wings into a formidable team again, making several deep playoff runs that included a return to the Stanley Cup Finals in 1995. It was in 1997 that Yzerman broke through, leading the Red Wings past the Philadelphia Flyers to win their first Stanley Cup in more than forty years. Yzerman would go on to help bring multiple Cups to Detroit, playing a major role in the title defense during the 1997–98 season, as well as the 2000–2001 victory. Yzerman retired in 2006—and he still holds the NHL record for most games as a captain.

> *Steve Yzerman has got this team in first place. People don't know about him yet, but he is battling Wayne Gretzky and Mario Lemieux for the scoring leadership in the NHL. Steve Yzerman is alive and well in Detroit.*
>
> —Red Wings coach Jacques Demers, 1988

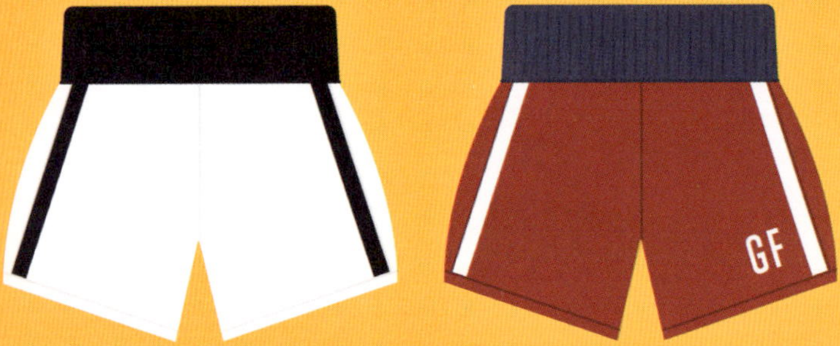
GF

Leading up to the fight, Ali garnered the support of the locals, adopting their chant of "Ali Bomaye!" which translates into "Ali, kill him!"

—

Shown on closed-circuit television in the United States, the fight actually took place at 4 a.m. local time.

—

The Rumble in the Jungle would become the subject of many films, songs, and writings, including the Academy Award–winning documentary *We Were Kings* and Norman Mailer's book *The Fight*.

Boxing

"THE RUMBLE IN THE JUNGLE"

George Foreman vs. Muhammad Ali

On October 30, 1974, Muhammad Ali fought the Heavyweight Champion of the World, George Foreman, in Kinshasa, Zaire (now Democratic Republic of the Congo). Ali was looking to regain the title he had lost in 1967 after being stripped of his belt for refusing to serve in the US Army. He had lost a previous title shot to Joe Frazier in 1971, then spent the next three years attempting to regain a title shot. Foreman entered the fight undefeated, having defended his title twice after beating Joe Frazier via technical knockout. The larger, stronger, and younger Foreman was favored to win. Both fighters had spent nearly a year training in Zaire, acclimating to the climate, and exchanging verbal barbs leading up to the fight. Once the fight started, Ali would employ what came to be known as the "Rope-a-Dope" technique, taking an onslaught of punches while pinned against the ropes, causing Foreman to tire himself out. Making his move in the eighth round, Ali was able to knock down the exhausted Foreman with a furious five-punch combination. Although Foreman rose to his feet after the count of nine, the referee called the fight. In what many consider to be one of the greatest bouts in boxing history, Ali regained his title at the age of thirty-two.

> *It will be a divine fight, a holy war... Armageddon on a miniature scale.*
>
> —Muhammad Ali

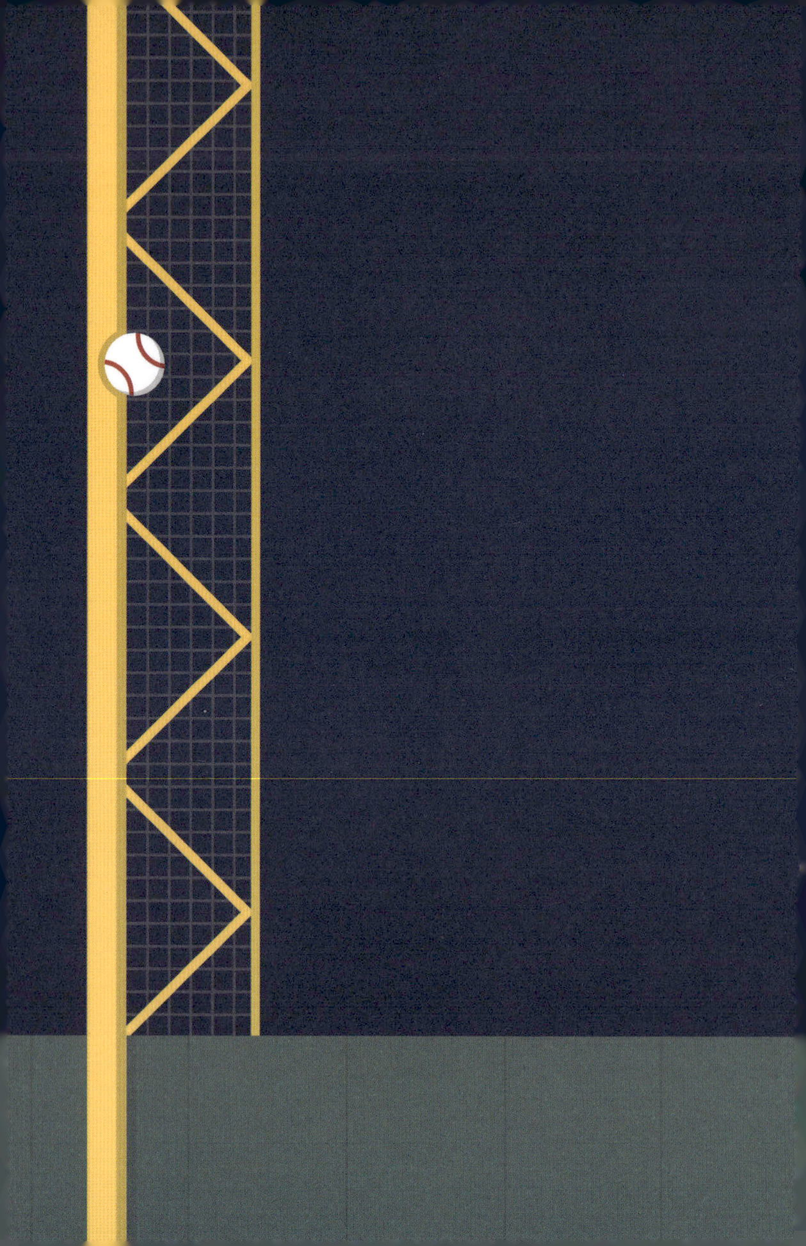

Each team in the Series had three future Hall of Famers on its roster: Johnny Bench, Joe Morgan, and Tony Perez for the Reds, and Fisk, Jim Rice, and Carl "Yaz" Yastrzemski for the Red Sox.

—

Reds pitcher Pat Darcy, who gave up the homer to Fisk, was the eighth pitcher Cincinnati used in the game.

Major League Baseball

CARLTON FISK
"Stay Fair!"

Considered one of the top offensive catchers of all time, Carlton Fisk enjoyed a Hall of Fame career, splitting his nearly twenty-five years in the majors between the Boston Red Sox and the Chicago White Sox. His most memorable moment would come as the Red Sox faced the Cincinnati Reds in the 1975 World Series. With the Sox facing elimination in Game 6, down 3 games to 2, the game headed to extra innings at Fenway Park. In the bottom of the twelfth, Fisk stepped to the plate with the game tied at 6 runs apiece. On the second pitch of his at-bat, Fisk crushed a ball down the left-field line, toward Fenway's famous Green Monster, but it appeared to be heading foul. Moving down the first-base line, Fisk frantically waved his arms to the right, pleading with the ball to stay fair. It would, as the ball hit off the foul pole and landed in left field, giving the Red Sox a victory in Game 6. A delirious Boston crowd celebrated while Fisk rounded the bases. Although the Red Sox would go on to lose Game 7 and the World Series, the image of a frenzied Fisk directing the ball fair remains one of the most iconic moments in World Series history.

> *It was probably as good a ball game as I've ever seen. A great game in a great series.*
>
> —Sparky Anderson, manager, Cincinnati Reds

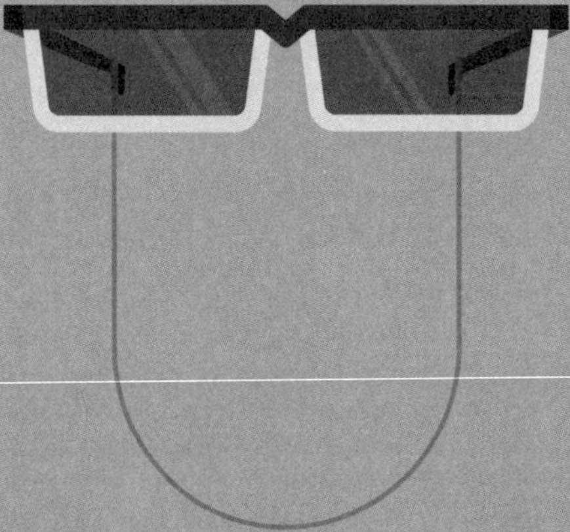

National Football League

AL DAVIS

"Just Win, Baby"

Davis hired the first Hispanic and African American head coaches in the history of the league, as well as being throughout his tenure an outspoken supporter of rules leading to more diversity in the game.

—

As the Raiders developed one of the most intense fan bases in the league, Davis once commented, "I will do anything for our fans, and it looks like they would do anything for this team."

—

Originally opposed to the AFL and NFL merging, Davis eventually played a key role in combining the two leagues, which forever changed the world of professional football.

One of the more colorful and controversial personalities in the history of football, Al Davis spent nearly sixty years in the game, as a coach, commissioner, and eventual owner and general manager of the Oakland Raiders. In his trademark tracksuit and dark sunglasses, Davis was always a fixture at Raiders practices, games, and press conferences. His personal motto of "Just win, baby" was reflected in the types of coaches and players Davis would bring to the Raiders over his tenure, including legendary coach John Madden, defensive end Howie Long, and cornerback Charles Woodson. He also ruled the organization with an iron fist, continually feuding with coaches, players, and members of the media. Davis was also tangled in several lawsuits with the NFL throughout his tenure, openly clashing with the commissioner's office, earning a reputation as a rogue within the NFL's circle of owners. Despite his prickly personality, the Raiders won three Super Bowls and fifteen division championships under his reign, and Davis was elected to the National Football Hall of Fame in 1992.

> *Once a Raider, always a Raider.*
> —Al Davis

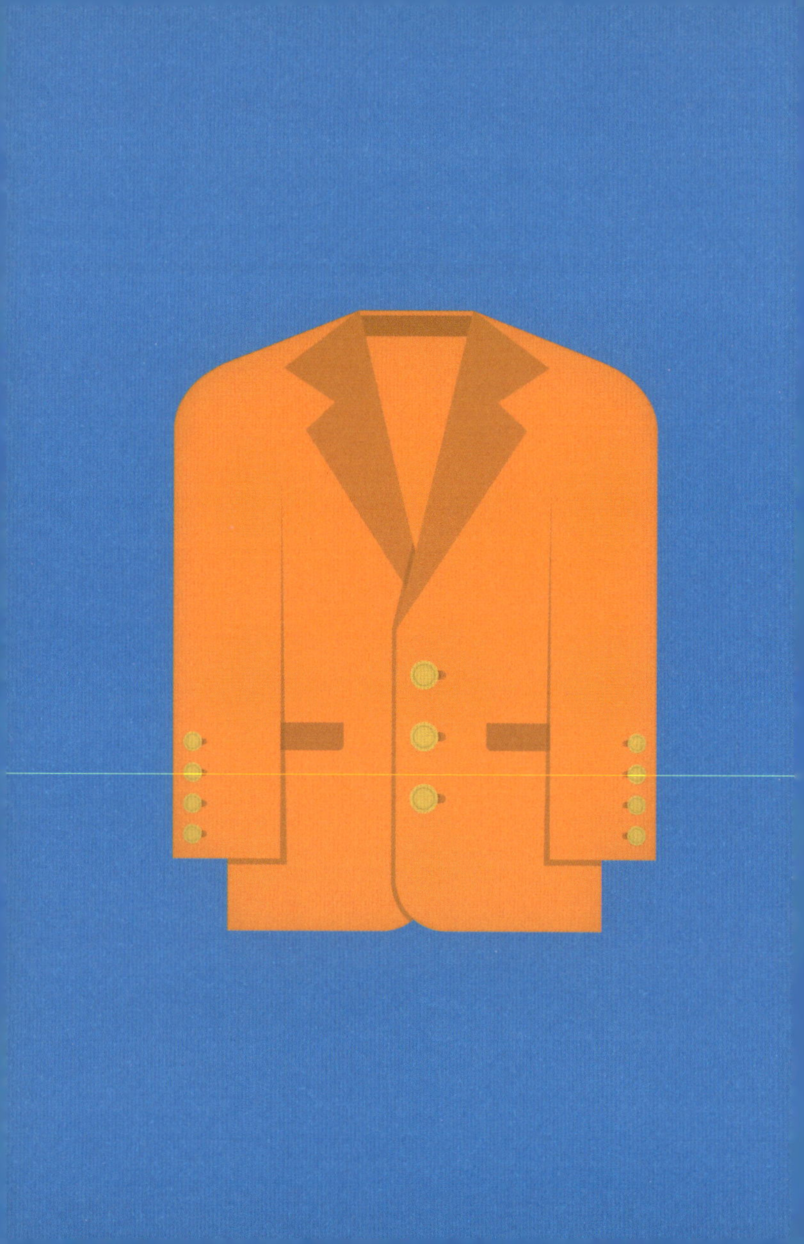

College Basketball

PAT SUMMITT
"Heart of the Lady Vols"

Summitt's 1,098 wins total is more impressive when you consider she only lost 208 games during that span, giving her an all-time winning percentage of .840.

—

Summitt developed an intense rivalry with UConn coach Geno Auriemma. As the two storied programs met and did battle numerous times over the years, Auriemma would liken the rivalry to that of the Yankees and the Red Sox.

—

In 2012, Summitt was awarded the Presidential Medal of Freedom, the highest civilian award given in the United States.

For nearly four decades, Pat Summitt continually set new standards of excellence as the coach of the women's basketball team at the University of Tennessee. After taking over the program as head coach in 1974, Summitt quickly turned the Lady Vols (for "Volunteers") into perennial contenders, being ranked number one in the country for the first time in 1978. Her mix of leadership, toughness, and intensity brought unprecedented success to the program, while also drawing attention to the women's game in general. Her achievements helped attract some of the best female players in history to attend Tennessee, including Candace Parker and Chamique Holdsclaw, further establishing the Lady Vols as the benchmark for women's college basketball. Patrolling the sidelines in her colorful suit jackets, Summitt led the team to 8 national championships in three different decades, along with 16 SEC championships, while also being named NCAA Coach of the Year eight times. Upon her retirement after 38 consecutive winning seasons, her 1,098 total wins are the most among any NCAA coach in history, male or female. She has since been elected to both the Women's Basketball Hall of Fame and the Naismith Memorial Basketball Hall of Fame.

> *I remember every player—every single one—who wore the Tennessee orange, a shade that our rivals hate.*
>
> —Pat Summitt

Tennis

BJÖRN BORG
"The Ice Man"

Borg was elected to the International Tennis Hall of Fame in 1987.

—

Borg's 11 Grand Slam singles titles rank him fifth all-time behind Roger Federer, Pete Sampras, Rafael Nadal, and Roy Emerson.

—

Borg attempted a comeback in the early 1990's, which resulted in disaster, as opponents routinely embarrassed him. Inexplicably, Borg attempted his comeback still using a wooden racket.

Björn Borg dominated tennis throughout the 1970's and '80's. Hailing from Sweden, his skill and stature would help popularize the game for a new generation of fans. He became a teenage sensation wearing his trademark headband, winning the French Open just weeks after his eighteenth birthday. Focusing on a powerful baseline game rather than the traditional serve-and-volley technique that ruled the game at that time, Borg embarked on an incredible run of success, at one point winning four consecutive French Opens and five consecutive Wimbledon titles. As his accomplishments grew more impressive, Borg developed an intense rivalry with John McEnroe, which famously culminated at the Wimbledon final of 1980. Borg defeated McEnroe after a grueling four-hour match, which featured an absurd 34-point tiebreaker. It is considered by many to be the best match in the history of the sport. Borg retired from tennis at age twenty-six in 1983, having already won 11 Grand Slam titles in just seven years. He still holds numerous records, perhaps most impressively having won nearly 90 percent of his Grand Slam singles matches throughout his career.

> *He was bigger than the game. He was like Elvis or Liz Taylor or somebody.*
>
> —tennis legend Arthur Ashe

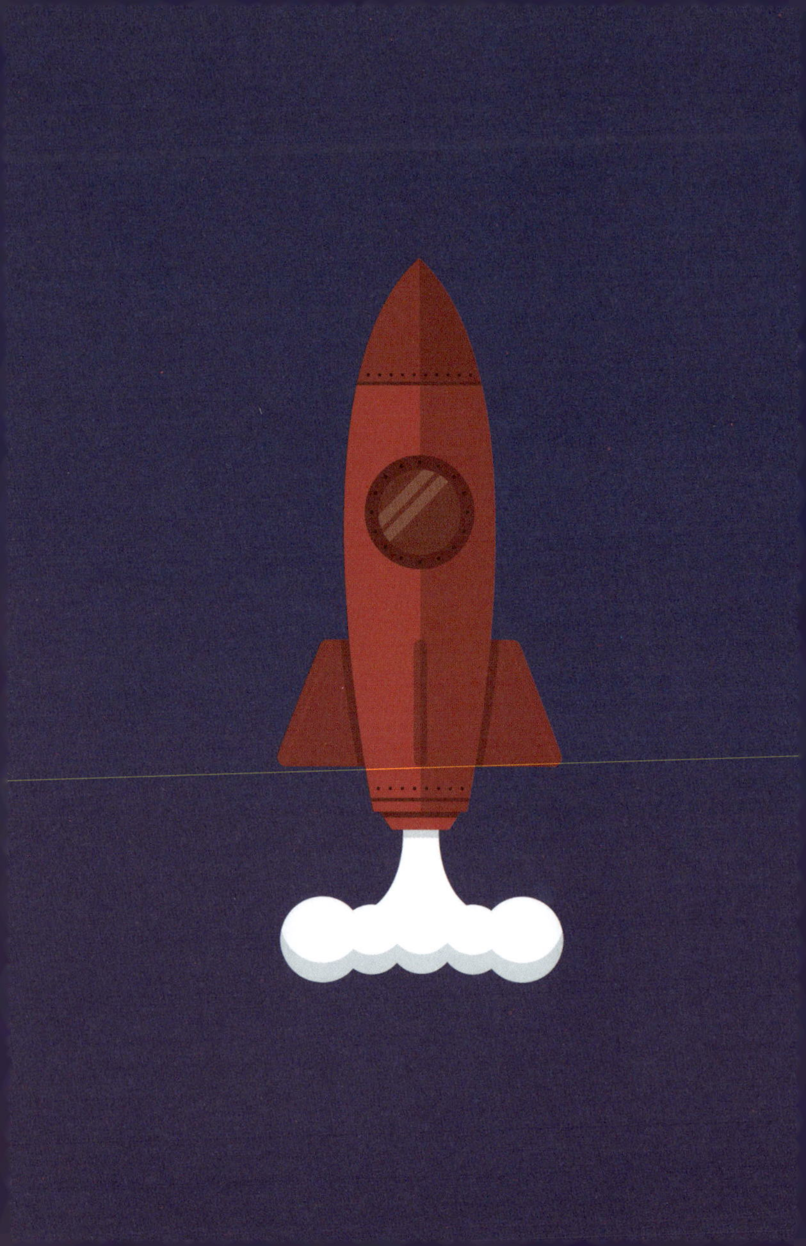

National Hockey League

MAURICE RICHARD
"Rocket"

Richard was elected to the Hockey Hall of Fame in 1961, just a year after he retired, as the NHL waived its standard five-year waiting period after retirement for a player to be eligible.

–

The "Richard Riot" became so intense and destructive that Richard himself had to take to the radio airwaves to calm the angry crowd.

–

Upon his death in 2000, Richard was honored with a state funeral in his native Quebec, the first for a nonpolitical figure in the history of the province.

Few players impacted the sport of hockey more than Maurice "Rocket" Richard did during his eighteen-year career with the Montreal Canadiens. Debuting during the 1942–43 season, he quickly earned his nickname for his ability to seemingly go from a standstill to full speed. Combining his speed with an equally incredible knack for finding the back of the net, Richard played an integral role in reviving the struggling Montreal franchise, winning eight Stanley Cups in three different decades. As a dominant goal scorer, he set numerous records during his career, including being the first player to score 50 goals in a season, first to 500 career goals, and retiring as the NHL's all-time goal-scoring leader (a mark later broken by Gordie Howe). As he developed into a superstar, the native of Montreal came to be so beloved by his city that fans rioted in protest after Richard was suspended for an altercation with a linesman in 1955. The legacy of this thirteen-time all-star and member of the Hockey Hall of Fame is still strong today, with the Maurice "Rocket" Richard Trophy awarded yearly to the NHL's top goal scorer.

> *When Maurice is worked up, his eyes gleam like headlights. Goalies have said he's like a car coming at you at night. He is terrifying.*
>
> —Frank Selke, Montreal Canadiens general manager

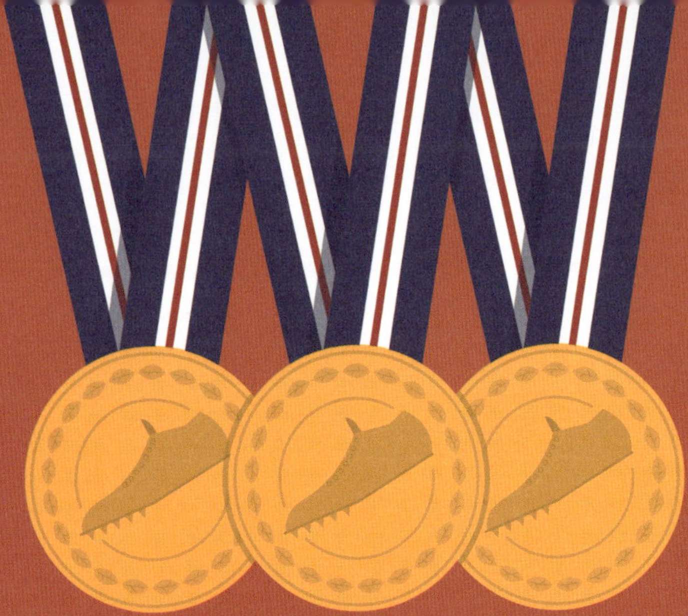

Olympic Track and Field
WILMA RUDOLPH
"Skeeter"

Her margin of victory was so great in the 200-meter race that the television cameras couldn't capture any of her competitors in the frame as she crossed the finish line.

—

Rudolph was named the Associated Press Woman Athlete of the Year in 1960 and 1961.

—

Thirty-four years later, Florence Griffith Joyner would become the second woman to win three gold medals in track and field, at the 1988 Olympic Games in Seoul; Joyner cited Rudolph as a major influence.

Through sheer determination, Wilma Rudolph would overcome near-impossible odds to become one of the most beloved Olympians in history. Wearing leg braces for most of her childhood, Rudolph suffered through multiple ailments, including bouts with scarlet fever and polio, at one point being told by a doctor she might never walk again. After a slow and steady recovery in her teenage years, Rudolph found her calling as an athlete, starring in both basketball and track while in high school, earning a track scholarship to Tennessee State. Her ability and performance while in college earned her a berth on the US Track and Field Team, where she won a bronze medal in 1956. But it was to be the 1960 Olympics in Rome when the world would find out what Rudolph was capable of. She became the star of the Games, winning the 100-meter and 200-meter sprints and 4×100 relay, becoming the first American woman to win three gold medals in a single Olympic Games. She instantly became a worldwide celebrity and was dubbed "the fastest woman in the world," a title she would carry through the 1960's. Upon returning to the United States after the Games, Rudolph and other Olympic athletes played a key role in the civil rights movement.

> *I don't know why I run so fast. I just run.*
> —Wilma Rudolph

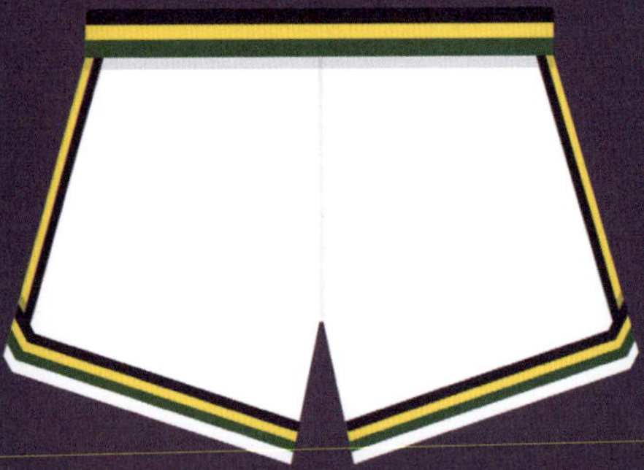

National Basketball Association

JOHN STOCKTON

"Stockton to Malone"

Stockton's record 15,806 assists are nearly four thousand more than the next highest total, belonging to Jason Kidd.

–

A testament to his durability, Stockton played in all 82 regular-season games in 16 of his 19 seasons.

–

Both Stockton and Malone played for the US Olympic team, winning gold medals in 1992 and 1996. Stockton wore his traditional number 12, while Malone chose to wear number 11, so the two could stand next to each other when receiving their medals.

For 19 seasons, John Stockton was one of the top point guards in the NBA. A diminutive six foot one, Stockton redefined the position in record-setting fashion. After playing his college career at the then little-known Gonzaga University, Stockton was drafted by the Utah Jazz in 1984. A gifted passer, defender, and shooter, Stockton established himself as the ultimate team player, doing whatever was needed to win, often sacrificing his body on screens against much larger, stronger players. When the Jazz drafted power forward Karl Malone in 1985, Stockton found a running teammate who made the pair one of the best one-two punches the league had ever seen. "Stockton to Malone" became synonymous with basketball in Utah for nearly two decades. As the league evolved around him, Stockton remained a throwback to an earlier era, all the way down to his shorts, which seemed to stay the same length his entire career. His consistent fundamental play earned him a place among the best point guards in history, making him a ten-time all-star and the NBA's all-time assists and steals leader.

> *John Stockton, to me, is the best that ever did it.*
> —Karl Malone

Major League Baseball

"THE MENDOZA LINE"

"The Mendoza line" spread across the sports world in the 1980's when ESPN's Chris Berman and others used the term during *SportsCenter* broadcasts.

—

Mendoza's best offensive season came in 1980, when he hit a respectable .245 playing for the Seattle Mariners.

—

A native of Mexico, Mendoza was elected to the Mexican Baseball Hall of Fame in 2000.

Mario Mendoza's career in the major leagues was by all accounts solid if not remarkable. As a shortstop, Mendoza played nine major-league seasons, putting in time with the Pittsburgh Pirates, Seattle Mariners, and Texas Rangers. Known for his prowess in the field, Mendoza struggled at the plate his entire career, a fact that overshadowed his defense and forever enshrined him in baseball lore. Although Mendoza had a .215 career average, .200 became the universal accepted mark of "The Mendoza line," considered the minimal acceptable threshold for a player's batting average. When a player approached or dipped below the Mendoza line, it was commonly seen as a mark of offensive futility. Just who coined the term is up for debate, since some have attributed its creation to Mendoza's Mariners teammates, and others to an interview Royals great George Brett gave in which he said, "The first thing I look for in the Sunday papers is who is below The Mendoza line." The term has made its way into other areas of society, including business and politics, but will most often be associated with the shortstop who could field but never really hit.

> *It did bother me, at the beginning, to be honest. Because people would come up to me, like making fun of me, so it used to make me mad, but now I don't care anymore.*
> —Mario Mendoza

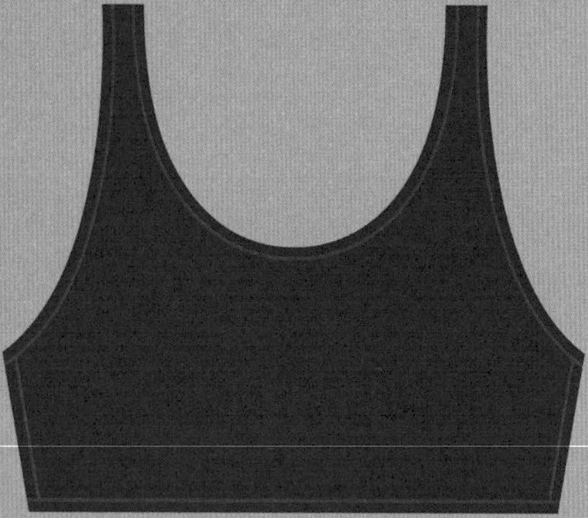

Soccer

BRANDI CHASTAIN

The 1999 women's final ranks third all-time in viewers for a US English-language soccer broadcast, with nearly 18 million viewers.

—

There was some controversy surrounding US goalkeeper Briana Scurry's technique during the shoot-out. Many claimed she had broken the rules several times by moving forward off the goal line before the Chinese struck their penalty kicks, including Liu Ying's. Goalkeepers are only allowed to move laterally in that situation, but no call was made by the referees.

The final of the 1999 Women's World Cup pitted the United States against China. In essence, it was a rematch of the final from the 1996 Olympics in Atlanta, where the United States had taken the gold medal and the Chinese the silver. Though both teams were evenly matched, the United States was favored to emerge victorious. In front of a crowd of more than 90,000, the teams met for the match in the Rose Bowl in Pasadena, California. After a full ninety minutes and a period of extra time, the teams were stuck in a scoreless tie and headed to a penalty kick shoot-out to decide the victor. The teams exchanged successful goals until Liu Ying missed on China's third attempt. The score was tied at 4–4 with only defender Brandi Chastain left to kick for the United States. Kicking left-footed, she was able to score top right, sealing the victory for the United States. In a spontaneous act, Chastain ripped off her jersey, revealing her black sports bra, and dropped to her knees in jubilation as her teammates rushed the field.

> *I remember the kick clearly. The celebration after was a whirlwind, a blur. The shock, frenetic energy when it happened, the team together jumping up and down, the stadium erupting.*
>
> —Brandi Chastain

← 🔔 →
BROAD ST

National Hockey League
"THE BROAD STREET BULLIES"
Philadelphia Flyers, 1973-75

In 1973, the Flyers became the first expansion franchise to win the Stanley Cup.

—

During the 1974-75 season, Schultz's record 472 penalty minutes were the equivalent of spending nearly eight full games in the penalty box.

—

Singer Kate Smith became the Bullies' good luck charm during their reign. The Flyers seemed to win whenever they played her rendition of "God Bless America" before home games. A tradition was born, and Smith was invited several times to sing in person, her animated performances receiving standing ovations from the Philadelphia crowds.

The Philadelphia Flyers of the 1970's were one of the meanest, toughest, most aggressive hockey teams ever assembled. After the team joined the NHL as an expansion franchise in 1967, Flyers ownership quickly realized they needed larger, stronger players to compete. The Flyers built a rogues' gallery of bruisers, including Dave "the Hammer" Schultz and Bob "Hound Dog" Kelly as the team's top enforcers, and center Bobby Clark as their best player and captain. The Broad Street Bullies (named for the street of their longtime home arena, the Spectrum) earned their nickname. Schultz set records in back-to-back years for most penalty minutes in a season. Fights and hard checking were the norm, and many opposing players came to fear playing the Flyers, especially in Philadelphia. By overpowering and intimidating their opponents, the Flyers became one of the top teams in the league. They won back-to-back Stanley Cups in 1973-74 and 1974-75, the first two and only championships in the franchise's history.

> *Let me say, first of all, that as a player your dad was not an angel.*
>
> —Dave Schultz, in a 1982 letter to his six-year-old son

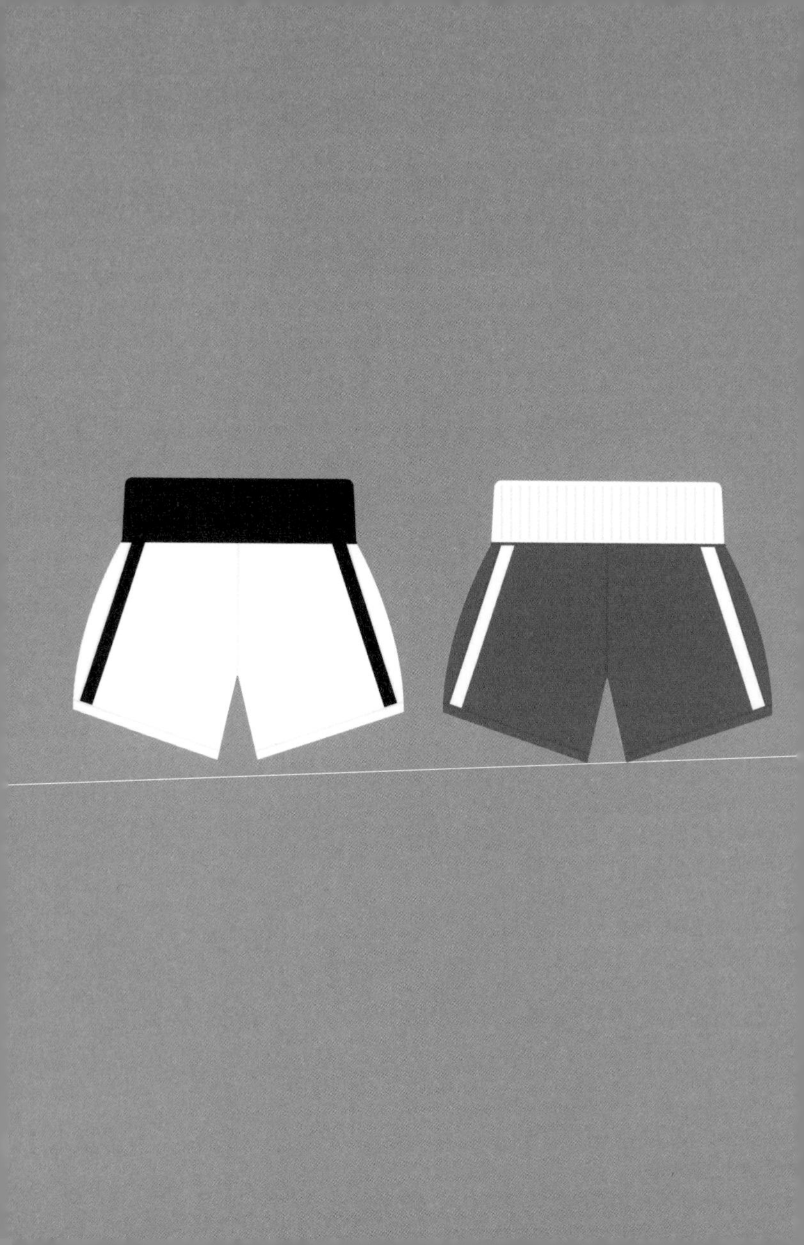

> The fight is considered by many to be the greatest boxing match in history.
>
> —
>
> After the fight, Ali would proclaim, "Joe Frazier is the greatest fighter in the world, next to me."
>
> —
>
> Following the fight, a shopping mall was built in the Philippines in honor of Ali's victory. Aptly named "Ali Mall," it remains open today.

Boxing

"THE THRILLA IN MANILA"

Muhammad Ali vs. Joe Frazier

October 1, 1975, would mark the third and final fight between heavyweights Muhammad Ali and Joe Frazier. With Frazier winning the first bout, and Ali the second, it was one of the most anticipated fights in history. Taking place in the Philippines, it was dubbed "The Thrilla in Manila" based on a rhyme Ali had recited at a prefight press conference, saying, "It's gonna be a chilla, and a killa, and a thrilla, when I get the Gorilla in Manila." The fight itself lived up to its billing. Ali, uncharacteristically aggressive, took the early rounds, attacking Frazier with several punch combinations. But Frazier stood tough and came back in the middle rounds, administering a vicious beating to Ali, and to many it appeared Frazier would have a clear advantage the rest of the fight. But in the late rounds, with Frazier tiring, Ali seized control. Digging to find whatever energy he could muster, Ali landed a flurry of punches. With Frazier's eyes nearly swollen shut from the beating he had taken, Frazier's trainer threw in the towel as the bell for the fifteenth and final round sounded. Frazier would later admit he basically fought blind the last few rounds. Both Ali and Frazier were gracious after the fight, praising each other for the physical and emotional beating they had both taken. Ali would say that the fight was the closest thing to dying he had every felt.

> *Man, I hit him with punches that'd bring down the walls of a city.*
>
> —Joe Frazier

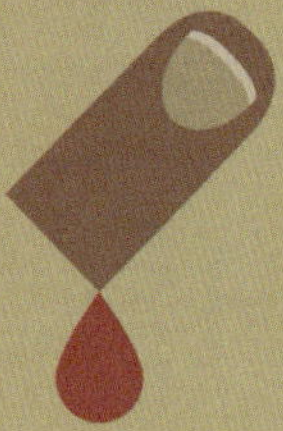

National Football League

RONNIE LOTT
"9½ Fingers"

Lott ranks ninth all-time in career interceptions with 63.

—

From 1981 to 1991, Lott was selected to the Pro Bowl ten times, only missing out in 1985, his first season at the safety position.

—

Known for the violence of his tackles, legendary coach Tom Landry said of Lott, "He's like a middle linebacker playing safety. He's devastating."

Ronnie Lott, one of the greatest defensive backs ever to play the game, commanded the San Francisco 49ers secondary for much of the 1980's, making the middle of the field a danger zone for any offensive player who came near him. After winning Super Bowls in 1981 and 1984, Lott made the switch to the safety position in 1985. During a tackle attempt that year, the tip of his left pinkie finger was crushed, and Lott was told he needed surgery to repair the damage. Rather than miss any games due to the recovery time needed after the operation, Lott chose to amputate the tip of his pinkie finger to assure a quicker return to the field. Lott's nine and a half fingers were good enough to help the 49ers win two more Super Bowls by the end of the decade. The decision cemented Lott as one of the toughest, and craziest, players in NFL history.

> *I'm going to have to let that finger go.*
> —Ronnie Lott to his doctors

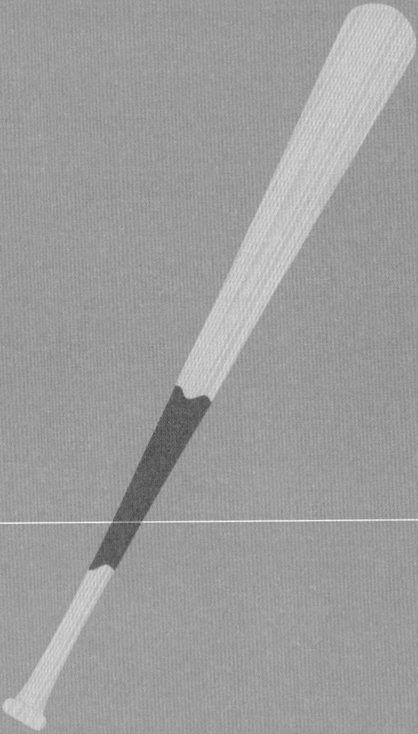

Major League Baseball

"THE PINE TAR INCIDENT"

Kansas City Royals vs. New York Yankees

One of the obscure rules in Major League Baseball concerns the use of pine tar, a sticky wood-based industrial by-product that players used to help improve their grip on their bats. The rule states that pine tar may not be used more than eighteen inches from the bottom of the bat. This rule was famously put to the test on July 24, 1983, at Yankee Stadium. George Brett, the veteran face of the Kansas City Royals, came up to bat in the top of the ninth inning, with two outs and the Royals trailing the Yanks, 4–3. Facing Yankee ace Goose Gossage, Brett hit what he thought was a go-ahead two-run home run to right field.

The Yankees' manager, Billy Martin, immediately protested Brett's home run. The home plate umpire Tim McClelland revoked the call, ending the game. Brett rushed the field to confront McClelland and was barely restrained by his teammates. The Royals vehemently protested the call. American League president Lee MacPhail reviewed the case and overturned the ruling. The home run was restored and the game resumed on August 18 from where it had left off (although Brett was retroactively ejected from the game for his outburst). The Yanks lost the game, 5–4.

> *To hit a home run off Goose was a big thrill, and then to have it taken away off a trivial portion of the rulebook, I just lost it. I looked like my father chasing me around after I brought home my report card.*
>
> —George Brett

MacPhail stated that the pine tar rule was based on economics, not batter advantage—if pine tar gets on a batted ball, it has to be removed from play, thus wasting too many balls.

–

Yankee Stadium charged non-season-ticket-holders $2.50 for entrance to the resumed game.

–

Martin played pitcher Ron Guidry at center field and first baseman Don Mattingly at second base to avoid having to use a pinch hitter.

–

As Filip Bondy related in his book *The Pine Tar Game*, Yankees owner George Steinbrenner said of MacPhail's ruling, "I would not want to be poor Lee living in New York City. He had better start house-hunting in Missouri, close to Kansas City."

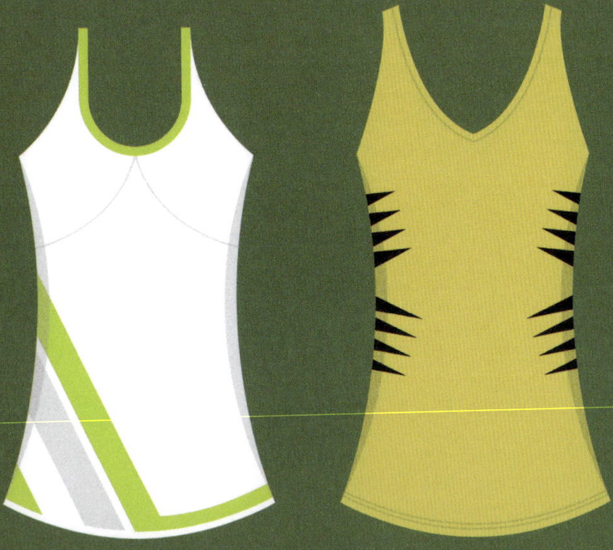

Tennis

2001 US OPEN FINAL
"Venus vs. Serena"

The siblings returned to Flushing, Queens, the next year and once again faced each other in the finals. The rematch went to Serena, who defeated Venus 6-4, 6-3.

—

Overall, the sisters have faced each other eight times in Grand Slam finals, with Serena winning six of those matches.

—

The sisters have had incredible success teaming up as doubles partners, winning thirteen Grand Slam titles, including five at Wimbledon.

As the only Grand Slam tennis tournament held in the United States, the US Open has had its fair share of great moments, and one of its crowning ones came in 2001 with the matchup of Venus and Serena Williams. The sisters landed on different sides of the draw at the tournament's start, and both made their way through their respective brackets to meet in the finals. It was the first time the Williams sisters faced each other in a Grand Slam final, as well as the first meeting between any siblings in tennis in more than one hundred years. It also marked the first time two African American women would square off in a Grand Slam final—an event so highly anticipated the match was the first women's final broadcast in prime time. On September 8, 2001, under the lights in Arthur Ashe Stadium, Venus defeated her younger sister in straight sets, 6-2, 6-4, and successfully defended her US Open title. It marked the beginning of a historic run for the Williams sisters, who would meet in seven more Grand Slam finals over the next several years.

> *I just don't like to see Serena lose against anybody—even me.*
>
> —Venus Williams

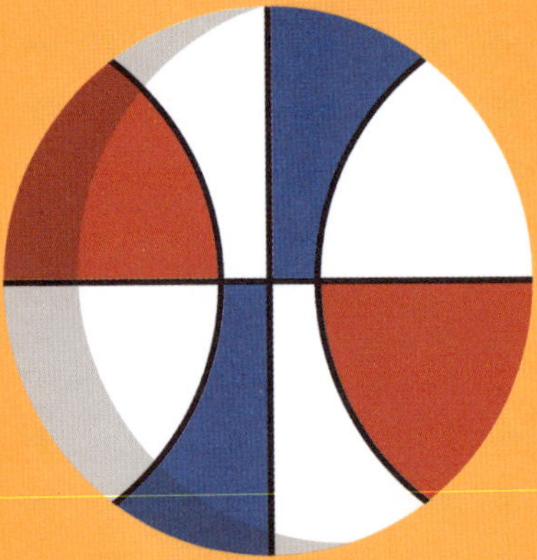

Professional Basketball League

AMERICAN BASKETBALL ASSOCIATION (ABA)

"Bring in the Funk"

The year 2003 would mark the first time two former ABA teams met in the NBA finals, with the San Antonio Spurs defeating the New Jersey (formerly New York) Nets.

—

As a testament to its talent level, all but one player to win the regular-season MVP award in the ABA has been elected into the Naismith Memorial Basketball Hall of Fame.

—

The lack of revenue faced by many ABA teams led to some interesting promotions, including "Halter Top Night," "Victor the Wrestling Bear," and a pregame concert by Glen Campbell.

For nine seasons in the culturally tumultuous late sixties and early seventies, the old, rigid guard of the NBA was challenged by the upstart American Basketball Association. The ABA offered up eleven regional teams and looser, faster play, as well as its signature red, white, and blue basketball. The ABA also had a new brand of star, personified in the likes of Julius "Dr. J" Erving, Connie Hawkins, and George Gervin, who thrilled fans with their energetic, freewheeling play. The ABA's 1976 All-Star Game was the first to feature a slam-dunk contest (won, of course, by Dr. J). What the ABA did lack was money—facing insolvency and with teams shuttering left and right, the ABA merged with the NBA at the end of the 1976 season. The Denver Nuggets, Indiana Pacers, New York Nets, and San Antonio Spurs were all absorbed by the NBA, with the remaining teams, like the Kentucky Colonels and the Virginia Squires, lost to history.

> *I keep both eyes on my man. The basketball hasn't moved on me yet.*
>
> —Julius "Dr. J" Erving

1.00

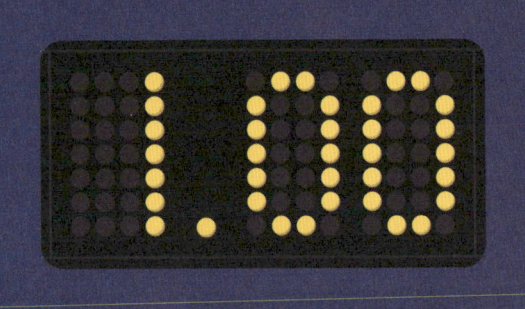

Olympic Gymnastics

NADIA COMANECI
"A Perfect 10"

As a fourteen-year-old Romanian gymnast, Nadia Comaneci was virtually unknown to the world heading into the 1976 Summer Olympics in Montreal. But she would leave the Games a global sensation, accomplishing what no other female gymnast had done before her. After a thrilling display on the uneven bars, Comaneci was awarded a perfect 10.0 by the judges, the first by a female gymnast in the history of the Olympics. The score was so unlikely that the special scoring system could not display a "10.0," her mark appearing as "1.00" instead. A stunned and delighted crowd erupted, their standing ovation bringing Comaneci back to the floor for a curtain call. She went on to record six more perfect scores during the Montreal games, taking home three gold medals in the all-around, uneven bars, and balance beam events. She became an international superstar and her achievements in that year's Games are credited with expanding interest and attention to the sport of gymnastics. She followed up her incredible 1976 performance with two more gold medals at the 1980 Games in Moscow before retiring from competition in 1981.

Comaneci was first discovered and trained by legendary coach Bela Karolyi, who would go on to coach the United States team.

-

Gymnasts Daniela Silivaș of Romania and Yelena Shushunova of the former Soviet Union would tie Comaneci's record of seven perfect scores at the 1998 Games in Seoul.

-

To the chagrin of many in the gymnastics community, a new scoring system introduced in 2006 had no ceiling, making a perfect 10.0 an impossibility.

> *A perfect ten for the first time!*
> —announcer and 1968 Olympiad Cathy Rigby

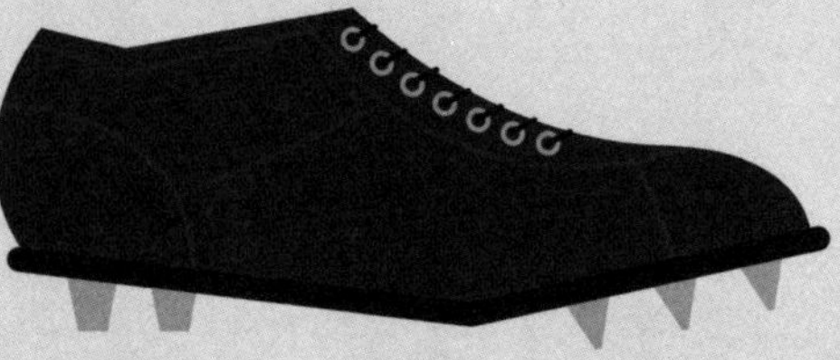

Major League Baseball

TY COBB
"Spikes Up"

Cobb was one of baseball's first superstars, playing nearly twenty-five seasons in the major leagues, twenty-two of which he spent with the Detroit Tigers. He was known as one of the fiercest and most aggressive competitors in the history of sport, as well as a bully. But there was no denying his sheer talent for baseball and his unstoppable drive. Cobb would use any advantage he could find, often leading members of opposing teams to accuse him of being a dirty player. Legend has it that he would sharpen his spikes to a point, intending to cause injury to opposing infielders when sliding into bases. Upon retiring after the 1928 season, he held more than forty major-league records, and in 1936 was one of the first players ever voted into the National Baseball Hall of Fame.

A very superstitious man, Cobb only signed autographs using green ink. He began the practice early in his career and continued it for the rest of his life.

—

Cobb won a record 12 batting titles, including 9 consecutive awards from 1907 to 1915. He finished his career with a lifetime average of .366, the highest in history.

—

As a testament to his intensity, famed baseball executive Branch Rickey said of Cobb, "He lived on the field as though it was his last day."

> *Second place didn't interest me.*
> —Ty Cobb

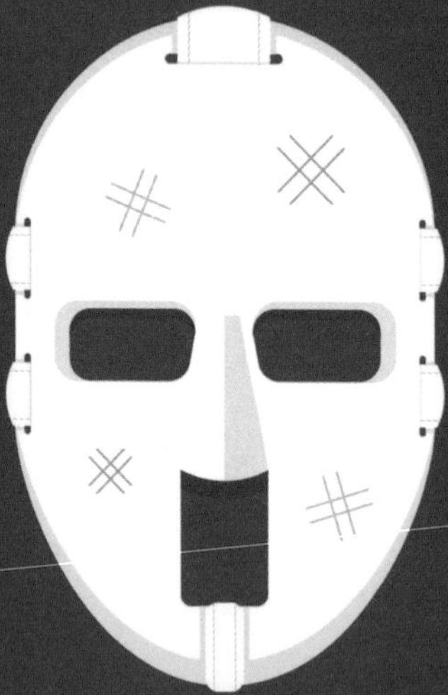

National Hockey League
JACQUES PLANTE
"Jake the Snake"

His 462 career wins rank him sixth among goaltenders all-time.

—

An accomplished and avid knitter, Plante was known for making his own underwear and knit caps.

—

The "Plante-style" mask was used throughout the 1960's, until masks with cages were introduced, which gave goaltenders a wider field of vision.

Jacques Plante literally changed the face of NHL goaltending. Over his twenty years of professional play, he helped win six Stanley Cups, earned a record seven Vezina Trophies, and was an eight-time all-star. His most visible contribution to the game came in 1959, when he became the first goaltender to wear a protective mask. Early that season, while minding the net for the Montreal Canadiens, Plante took a slapshot to the face during a game against the New York Rangers, breaking his nose. After being stitched up in the locker room, Plante returned to the ice wearing a homemade protective mask, much to the ire of his coaches. At the time, wearing a mask was considered a sign of weakness, as well as being against the tradition of the game. Undeterred, Plante continued to wear his mask, refining the design and making adjustments along the way. By the 1970's goaltenders donning colorful masks were the norm, adding personal style and flair to the game that continue to this day.

> *If I don't wear the mask, I'm not playing.*
> —Jacques Plante

W	L
𝍸 𝍸	
𝍸 𝍸	
𝍸 𝍸	
𝍸 𝍸	
𝍸 𝍸	
𝍸 𝍸	
𝍸 𝍸	
𝍸 |||	

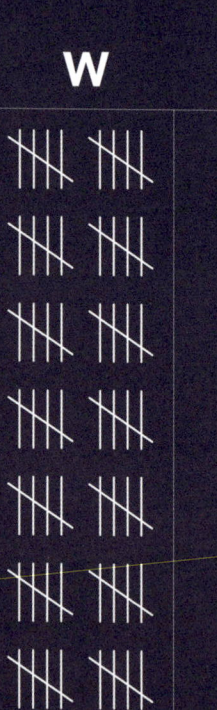

Amazingly, the 2009-10 team won every game by more than 10 points. Stanford came closest to defeating the Huskies that season, losing by 12 points.

—

The streak would continue into the 2010-11 season, eventually reaching 90 games before UConn was defeated by Stanford, 71-59.

—

Maya Moore was selected first overall in the 2011 WNBA Draft, winning Rookie of the Year honors playing for the Minnesota Lynx.

College Basketball

2008–10 UCONN WOMEN'S BASKETBALL

"Undefeated"

The University of Connecticut Huskies, led by beloved coach Geno Auriemma, have long been one of the standout teams in women's college basketball, with several championship stints, but never more so than during the 2008-9 and 2009-10 seasons. Heading in to the 2008-9 season, UConn was expected to be among the nation's best teams, but it's safe to assume no one could have predicted just how good they would be over the next two years. With a roster that featured stars like Tina Charles and Maya Moore, the Huskies went two full seasons without a loss en route to consecutive national championships. In 2008-9, they would finish the season 39-0, defeating the University of Louisville in the NCAA women's final. Not missing a beat in 2009-10, they would again finish at 39-0, defeating Stanford University in the championship game. Ending their two-season run at 78-0, they would set a new precedent in collegiate sports, becoming the first Division I women's basketball team to finish undefeated while winning back-to-back championships.

> *She's kind of like a legend, like a blockbuster movie.*
> —Coach Geno Auriemma, on Tina Charles

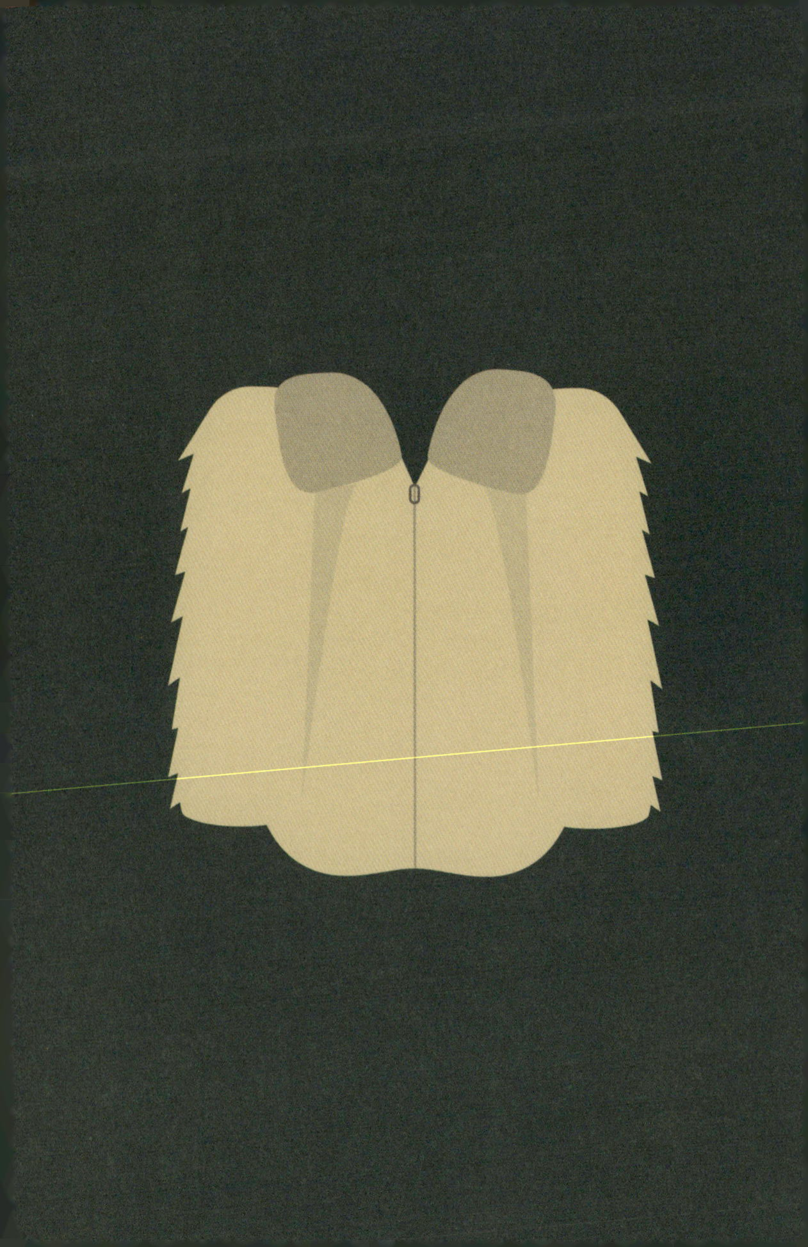

National Football League

JOE NAMATH
"Broadway Joe"

Namath was also drafted by the St. Louis Cardinals of the NFL, but chose to sign with the Jets in 1965. The AFL and NFL would merge before the 1970 season.

–

Namath remains the Jets' all-time leader in wins, passing yards, and touchdowns at the quarterback position.

–

Before Super Bowl III, the Colts were favored by up to 18 points, making the Jets' victory one of the biggest upsets in Super Bowl history.

After Joe Namath led the University of Alabama to a national championship in 1964, the New York Jets selected him with the first pick in the American Football League (AFL) draft. Halfway through his rookie year, Namath would take over as Jets starting quarterback, a role he would thrive in over the next decade. Earning the nickname "Broadway Joe," he was considered football's first superstar. In many ways Namath, often seen at the trendiest spots in New York, or wearing a fur coat along the sideline during a game, personified the celebrity athlete. Namath also made headlines on the field, becoming the first quarterback in history to throw for 4,000 yards in a season, as well as a four-time all-star. He is perhaps best known for his prediction of victory before Super Bowl III, versus the heavily favored Baltimore Colts, led by the legendary quarterback Johnny Unitas. Namath led the Jets to victory, famously holding up a single finger in celebration while running off the field after the game. Injuries would eventually hinder Namath's productivity in his later years, but he remains synonymous with football in New York City.

> *We're gonna win the game. I guarantee it.*
> —Joe Namath, before Super Bowl III

K

Major League Baseball

NOLAN RYAN
"The Ryan Express"

As an intimidating, hard-throwing right-hander who routinely topped 100 miles an hour with his fastball, Nolan Ryan pitched for an amazing 27 seasons in the major leagues. Over his career Ryan spent time with the New York Mets, Houston Astros, California Angels, and Texas Rangers. He holds two pitching records that will most likely never be broken: Upon his retirement, he had racked up an amazing 5,714 career strike-outs, nearly 900 more than Randy Johnson, the next-closest player. Ryan tossed 7 no-hitters, also an all-time record. As a testament to his longevity and durability, he threw a no-hitter in three different decades, as his first and last no-hitters came a staggering eighteen years apart. His first was recorded on May 15, 1973, as he no-hit the Kansas City Royals as a member of the Angels. His last was on May 1, 1991, as he no-hit the Toronto Blue Jays as a member of the Texas Rangers. Beloved by fans and teammates, he remains the only player in baseball history to have his number retired by three different teams.

In addition to throwing 7 no-hitters, Ryan tossed 12 one-hitters in his career, tied for most all-time with Bob Feller.

–

Ryan would soak his fingers in pickle juice between starts to avoid getting blisters.

–

Reggie Jackson said of Ryan: "He was the only guy that could put fear in me. Not because he could get me out, but because he could kill me."

> *It helps if the hitter thinks you're a little crazy.*
> —Nolan Ryan

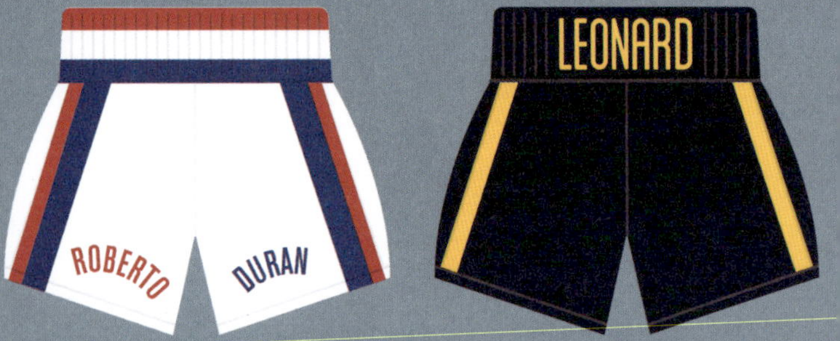
ROBERTO
DURAN
LEONARD

Boxing

"NO MÁS"

Roberto Duran vs. Sugar Ray Leonard

Duran would repeat several times over the years that he never said *"No más."* He accused legendary broadcaster Howard Cosell of making up the whole thing. Referee Octavio Meyran has consistently maintained he heard Duran utter the famous words.

—

In the wake of the fight, trainer Ray Arcel would part ways with Duran, saying, "Nobody quits in my corner."

—

Duran had his purse from the fight suspended and was fined $7,500 for his "nonperformance."

Roberto Duran and Sugar Ray Leonard faced each other three times during their careers, but it was their second fight that stands as one of the most infamous moments in the history of the sport. During their first bout, in Montreal's Olympic Stadium in July 1980, Leonard had abandoned his quick, weaving style, instead trying to slug it out with Duran, who won that first meeting by decision, taking the WBC Welterweight Championship from Leonard. The rematch was scheduled for five months later, at the Louisiana Superdome on November 25, 1980. As the bout unfolded, Leonard returned to his traditional style, landing numerous punches while Duran struggled to find his footing. Near the end of the seventh round, Leonard landed a strong left jab to Duran's face, prompting him to turn his back on the fight and utter two of the most famous words in boxing history: "No más." No more. The fight was stopped and Leonard won back his WBC title by technical knockout. The boxing world was stunned, since Duran, with "Fists of Stone," was known as one of the toughest and most dedicated fighters in the sport. Duran would later claim he had thrown in the towel due to injury, which was met with great skepticism, and his reputation took a severe hit. "No más" remains one of the most unexpected conclusions to a fight in the history of boxing.

> *I am retiring from boxing right now. I don't want to fight anymore.*
>
> —Roberto Duran, after the fight

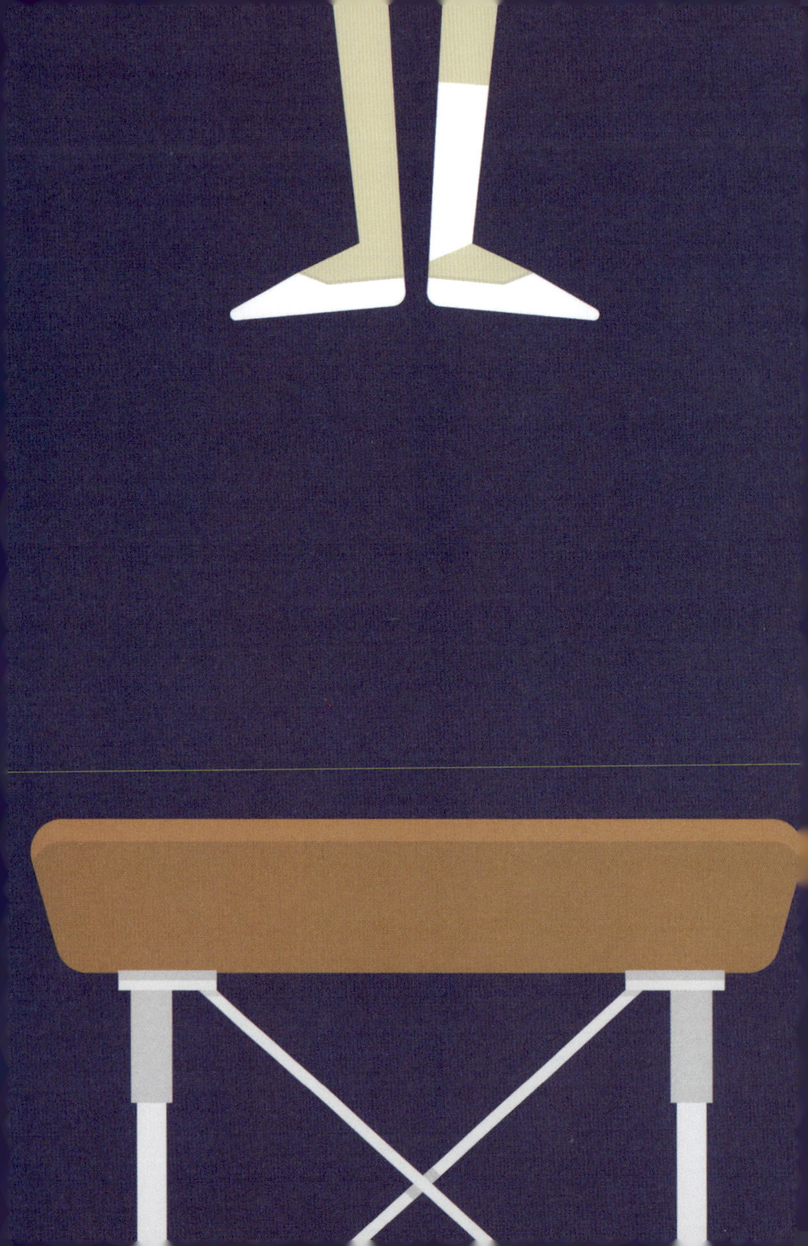

Strug's score of 9.721 on her final attempt won the gold medal by the slimmest of margins, pushing the Americans a mere .821 points ahead of the Russians.

—

Leading up to the 1996 Games, the former Soviet Union had won the gold medal in the women's team event 11 of the 12 previous Olympics, dating back to 1952. The lone year they did not win was 1984, when the Soviets, along with several other nations, boycotted the Olympic Games in Los Angeles.

—

Overall, the United States dominated the 1996 Games, winning a total of 101 medals, 44 of which were gold. The next-closest country was Germany, with 65 total medals.

Olympic Gymnastics

KERRI STRUG
"One More Try"

Heading into the 1996 Summer Olympics in Atlanta, the United States women's gymnastics team had never won the gold medal in the team event. Many thought this would be the year for the US women. Nicknamed "the Magnificent Seven," the team's talented roster included Dominique Dawes, Shannon Miller, and Dominique Moceanu. After the uneven bar, floor, and balance beam events, the United States held a commanding lead over Russia. With only the vault event remaining, a gold medal for the United States looked assured. But the Americans struggled mightily, most notably Moceanu, who fell twice during her attempts. Shockingly, the gold medal was up for grabs, as the Russians had steadily made up ground in their final event, the floor. The gold would be decided by Kerri Strug, the last team member to vault for the United States. On her first attempt, Strug missed her landing, falling and badly injuring her ankle, not scoring well enough to secure the gold. On her heavily taped and injured ankle, a hobbled Strug stuck the landing on her second vault attempt, lifting her injured ankle while saluting the judges, securing the gold medal for the United States. Unable to walk afterward, Strug was carried to the medal podium by coach Bela Karolyi, capping off one of the gutsiest performances in Olympic history.

> *People think these girls are fragile dolls. They're not. They're courageous.*
>
> —US gymnastics coach Bela Karolyi

85

5

College Football

"THE FIFTH DOWN"

Colorado vs. Missouri, October 6, 1990

Many have attributed the confusion to the fact that 1990 was the first year in which offenses were allowed to spike the ball to stop the clock.

—

The controversial victory was reflected in the poll rankings the following week, as Colorado fell from number 12 to number 14.

—

A similar error happened in 1940 during a matchup between Dartmouth and Cornell. Late in the game, Cornell was given an extra down after failing to score near the Dartmouth goal line. They would use the extra down to score a touchdown and win the game, though Cornell would later forfeit its victory.

The 1990 matchup between the University of Missouri and the University of Colorado, played at Missouri's Faurot Field, was a close affair throughout. Down 31–27 late in the fourth quarter, Colorado drove deep, finding itself with a first and goal from the one yard line with just over half a minute remaining. Colorado quarterback Charles Johnson spiked the ball on first down, stopping the clock. On second down, a run attempt was stopped short of the goal line, prompting Colorado to call its last timeout. When the teams lined up to run the third-down play, the down markers along the sideline had not been changed from second to third down. No one seemed to notice the error. Colorado tried to run the ball but was stopped short of the goal line, as the clock continued to run. With the down markers now showing third instead of fourth down, Johnson spiked the ball to stop the clock with just seconds remaining. On the "fifth" down, Johnson kept the ball and crossed the goal line to win the game. The officiating crew soon realized their mistake, but ruled that the score would count, and Colorado won the game 33–31. The incredible blunder and controversial victory proved to be critical, as Colorado would win the rest of its games, earning a share of the national title with Georgia Tech.

I got sick to my stomach just thinking about it.
—Rich Montgomery, official in charge of the down markers

87

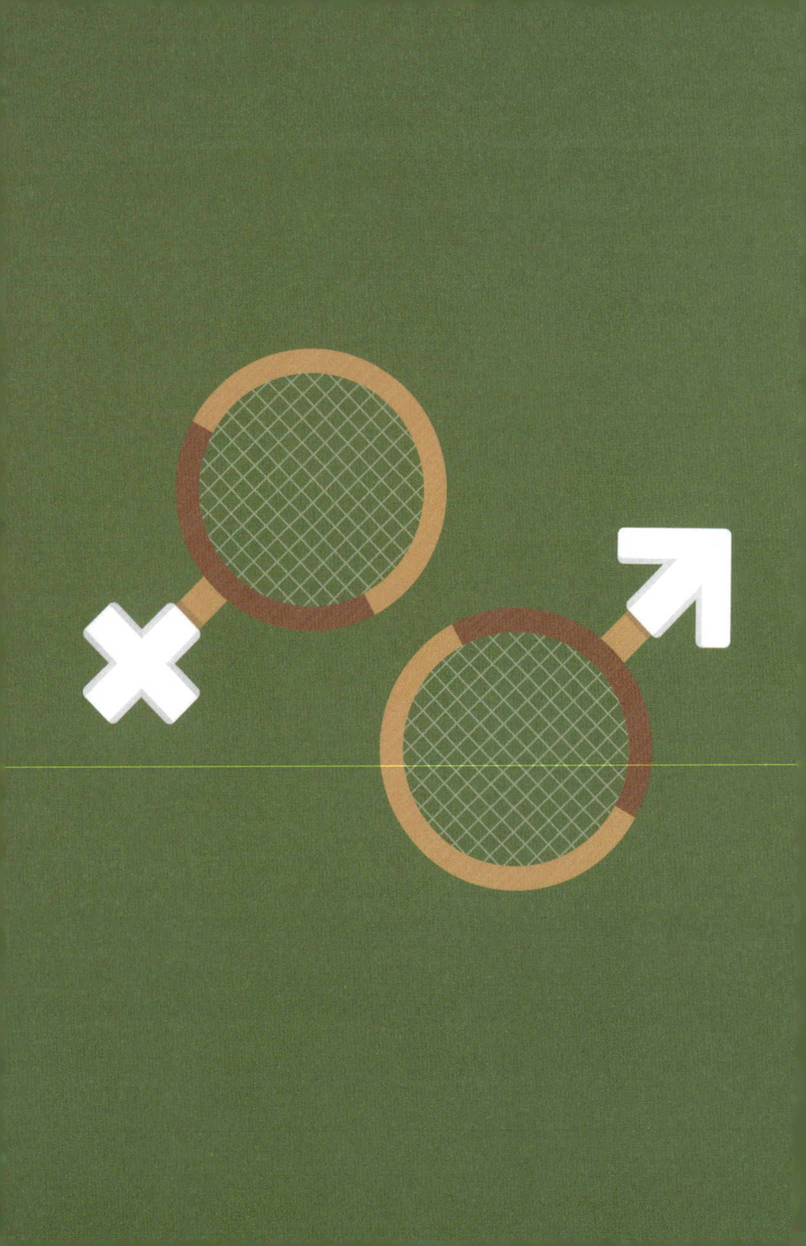

Riggs's first coed match, against Margaret Court, took place on May 13, 1973. It was so one-sided it was dubbed "The Mother's Day Massacre," as Riggs won 6–2, 6–1.

-

Rumors surfaced that Riggs had thrown the match against King in exchange for the forgiveness of his gambling debts.

Tennis

"THE BATTLE OF THE SEXES"

Billie Jean King vs. Bobby Riggs

One of the top male tennis players of the 1940's, Bobby Riggs had been out of the spotlight for some time when Billie Jean King rose to become one of the top female tennis stars in the 1960's and 1970's. A consummate showman and promoter of the game, Riggs claimed that at age fifty-five he could still beat the top female players, and challenged the twenty-nine-year-old King to an exhibition match. King initially declined, but later accepted after Riggs had defeated Margaret Court, another top female player. Leading up to their match, Riggs continued to unleash a slew of insults about women's tennis and women in general, which resulted in the match being dubbed "The Battle of the Sexes." A crowd of more than 30,000 gathered in the Houston Astrodome on September 20, 1973, at that time a record number of spectators for a tennis match. It was also broadcast on national television, and King beat Riggs handily in straight sets, 6–4, 6–3, 6–3.

> *I underestimated you.*
> —Bobby Riggs to Billie Jean King

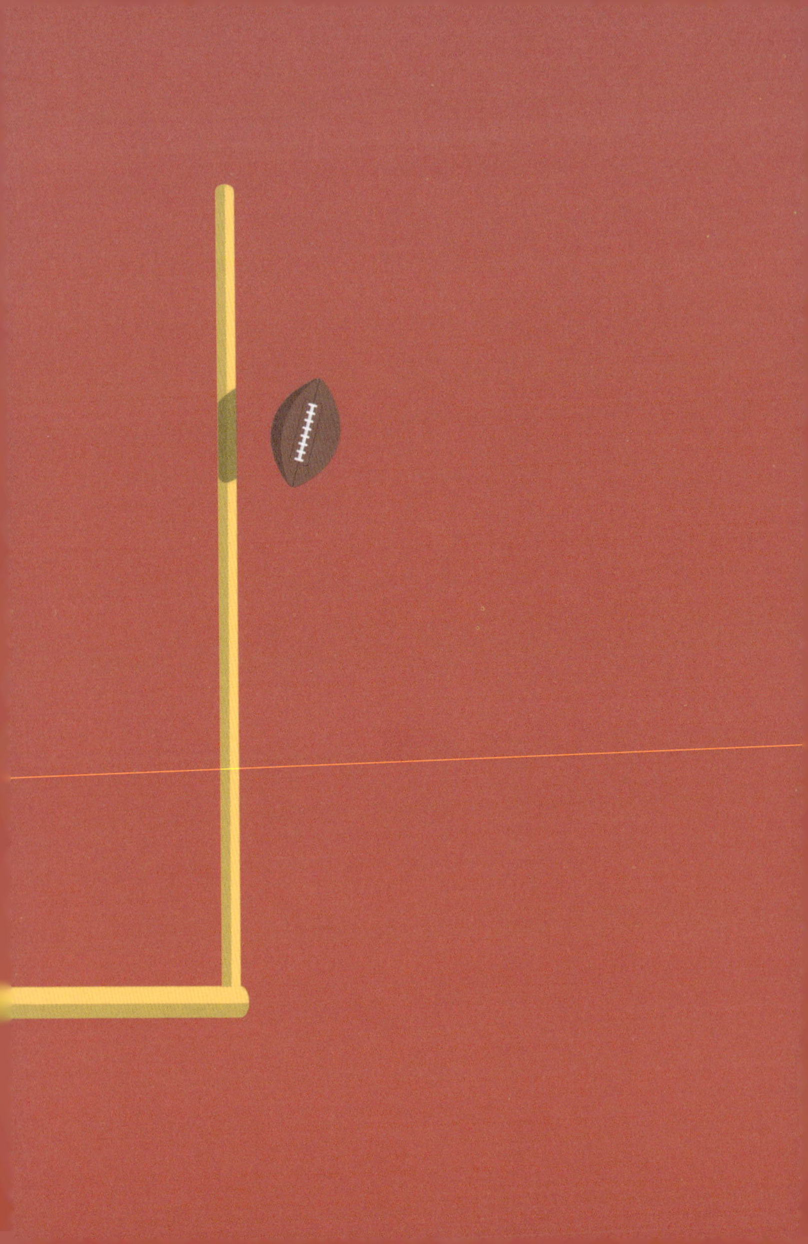

National Football League

SCOTT NORWOOD
"Wide Right!"

Super Bowl XXV was played in Tampa, Florida, on January 27, 1991. The game pitted the Buffalo Bills against the New York Giants. With both teams ending their regular seasons at 13-3, the highly anticipated game did not disappoint. The Bills trailed 20–19 with eight seconds left in the fourth quarter but found themselves with a chance to win the game with a field-goal attempt by kicker Scott Norwood. The previous limit of Norwood's range was forty-seven yards; this kick—for the game—would be from . . . forty-seven yards. Norwood's kick went, as commentator Al Michaels exclaimed, "wide right!" The brutal defeat would mark the beginning of an unprecedented four straight Super Bowl losses for Buffalo.

Norwood hadn't exactly had a stellar year before the Super Bowl, making only 20 of 29 field-goal attempts during the regular season.

–

Norwood would return to the Bills in 1991, but was waived after the season and never kicked in the NFL again.

–

Super Bowl XXV was one of two Super Bowls in which neither team committed a turnover. The other was Super Bowl XXXIV, in 2000, as the St. Louis Rams defeated the Tennessee Titans.

The Super Bowl will ride on the right foot of Norwood.
—Buffalo radio announcer Van Miller, awaiting the snap

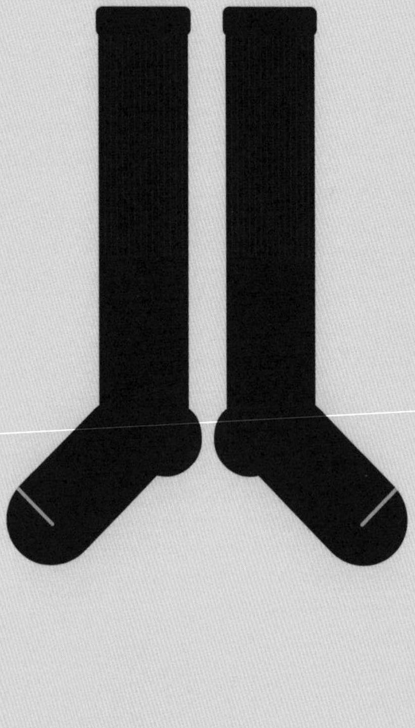

College Basketball

THE FAB FIVE

University of Michigan Wolverines, 1991-93

Despite the fact that they never won an NCAA championship, the 1991 recruiting class of the University of Michigan is considered one of the best, and certainly one of the most influential, teams in the history of both college and professional basketball. The team's centerpiece was a group of five players with incomparable talent, brash attitude, and distinct fashion sense: Chris Webber, Jalen Rose, Juwan Howard, Jimmy King, and Ray Jackson, known collectively as "the Fab Five." Within a few years of their ascendancy, their shaved heads, baggy shorts, and high black socks became de rigueur NBA fashion, moving away from both the look and the more reserved style of play of previous generations. With the Fab Five on the court, Michigan reached the NCAA championship in back-to-back years (losing to Duke and North Carolina respectively), and it remains the only team to start five freshmen in a championship game.

The end of the 1993 championship game versus North Carolina will forever be remembered for Webber calling a timeout when the Wolverines had none remaining, resulting in a technical foul and sealing the win for the Tar Heels.

–

Four of the Fab Five would go on to play in the NBA, with Ray Jackson the only member never playing in the league.

–

In 2002, an NCAA investigation into longtime Michigan booster Ed Martin and his practice of giving money to players resulted in the university vacating the Fab Five's 1992 and 1993 Final Four runs, among other sanctions.

> *It was the bling-bling era. We wore two chains, two bracelets, one watch. Our clothes were oversized. We did everything big. Bigger.*
>
> —Jalen Rose

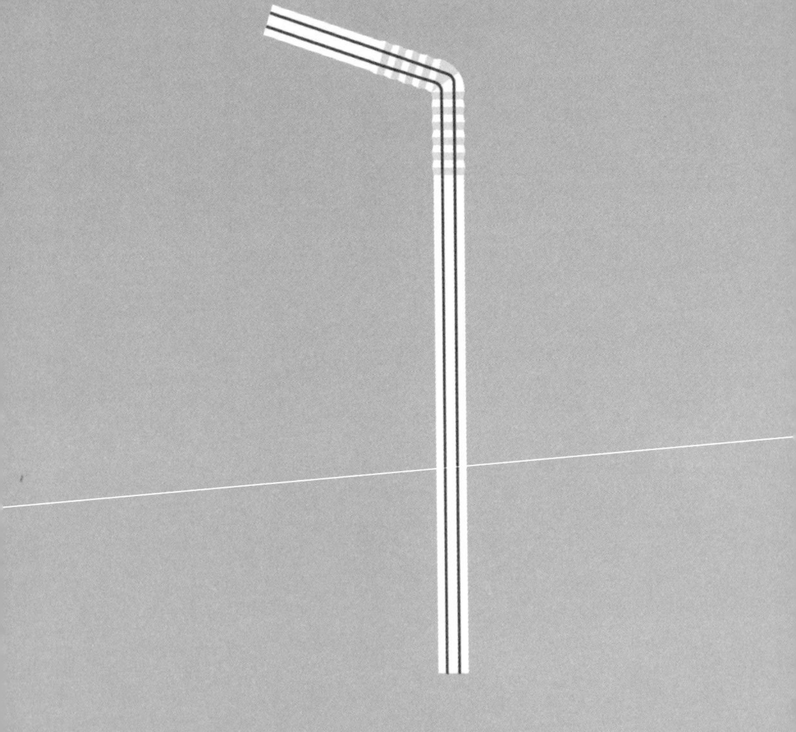

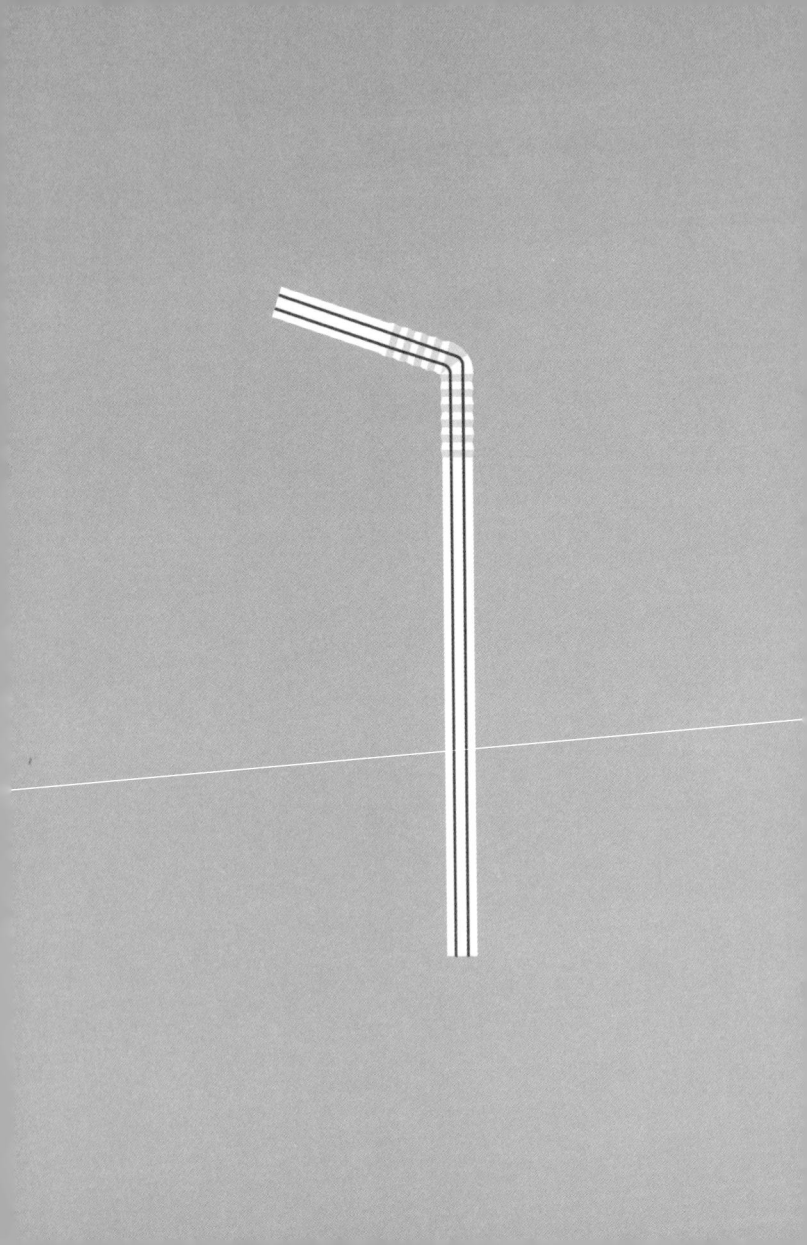

Major League Baseball

REGGIE JACKSON
"The Straw That Stirs the Drink"

Jackson was dubbed "Mr. October" by teammate Thurman Munson.

—

Before Game 2 of the 1977 Series, a fire broke out in an abandoned school close to Yankee Stadium, prompting famed sports announcer Howard Cosell to announce during the game's television broadcast, "There it is, ladies and gentlemen. The Bronx is burning."

—

Despite hitting 563 home runs in his career, Jackson remains the all-time strikeout leader, fanning a record 2,597 times.

After winning three consecutive World Series with the Oakland Athletics and spending a year with the Baltimore Orioles, right fielder Reggie Jackson signed as a free agent with the New York Yankees in 1977. While team ownership was excited about Jackson's arrival, Yankees manager Billy Martin and the Yankee players were not as enthused. Any goodwill Jackson might have had was further soured by an interview in *SPORT* magazine that Jackson gave during spring training. "This team, it all flows from me," Jackson said. "I'm the straw that stirs the drink." Jackson would later insist his quote was taken out of context, but by then the damage was done. Jackson clashed with Martin and his teammates throughout the year, mainly over Jackson's perceived lack of hustle and effort. Despite the turmoil, the Yankees were able to make it to the World Series. While playing the Los Angeles Dodgers, Jackson would prove he was indeed the straw that stirred the drink, hitting three home runs in consecutive at-bats in a decisive Game 6 victory, sealing the World Series for the Yankees.

> *God, do I love to hit that little round son of a bitch out of the park and make 'em say "Wow!"*
>
> —Reggie Jackson

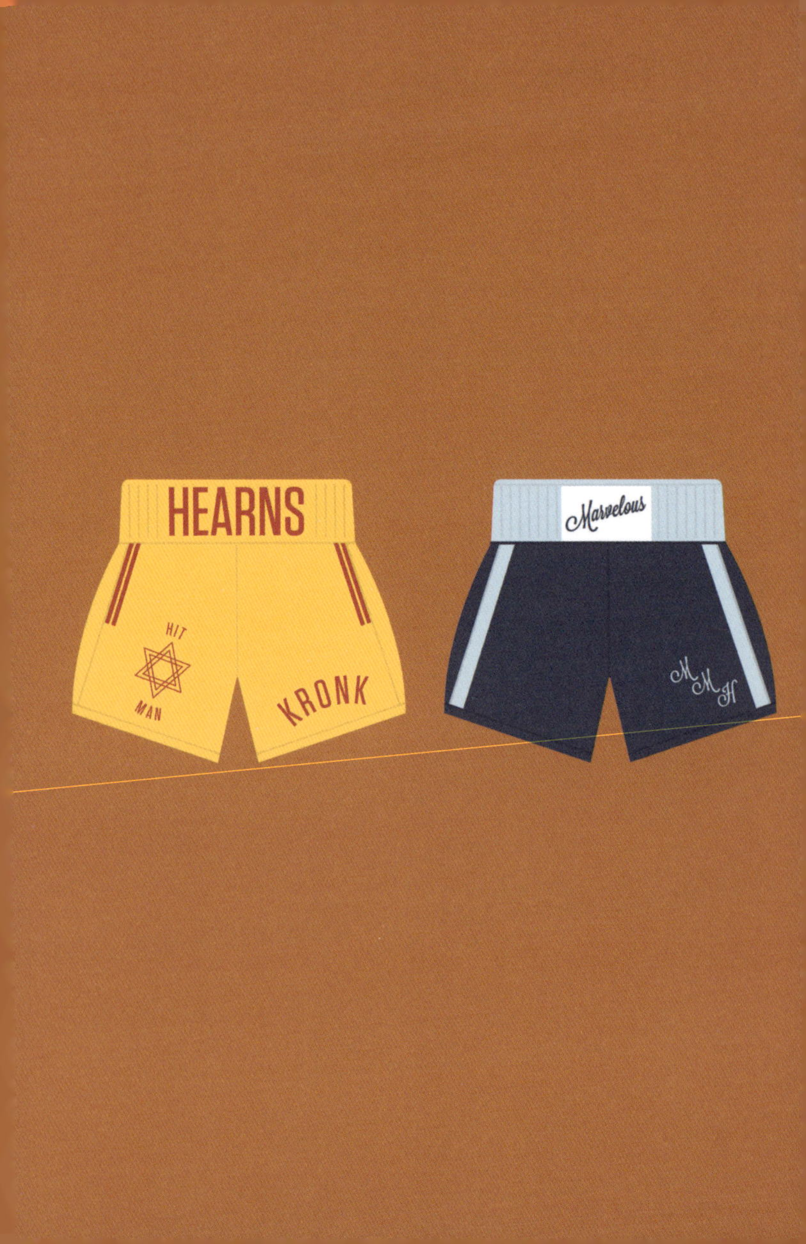
HEARNS
HIT
MAN
KRONK
Marvelous
MMH

Boxing

"THE WAR"
Thomas Hearns vs. Marvin Hagler

"The War," as it would later become known, is one of the most violent fights in the history of boxing. On April 15, 1985, Thomas "Hit Man" Hearns met "Marvelous" Marvin Hagler at Caesars Palace in Las Vegas. At the time, Hagler was the undisputed Middleweight Champion of the World, having defended his title successfully several times. An eager, younger Hearns had moved up in weight class to challenge Hagler. The promotion and buildup to the fight between two men considered to be among the best fighters of their time was intense, but it was nothing compared to the actual bout. What followed the opening bell was three rounds of absolute mayhem, as both fighters came out incredibly aggressive, swinging and connecting rapidly. As they traded vicious blows, the violent intensity of the fight was shocking. Hagler eventually caught a tiring Hearns with a succession of uppercuts, ending the fight before the close of the third round. Hagler finished the fight with a face covered in blood from a cut across his forehead, and Hearns was carried to his corner by his trainers after the fight was stopped after only eight minutes.

Ring magazine named "The War" the fight of the year in 1985, later declaring the first round to be the best of the twentieth century.

—

Hagler switched stances during the fight, alternating between orthodox and southpaw styles, allowing him to pin Hearns several times along the ropes.

—

Hearns's trainer, Emanuel Steward, suspected that a prefight massage had weakened Hearns's legs, causing him to change his strategy during the bout.

> *That was an entire fight encompassed in three minutes.*
> —announcer Al Michaels

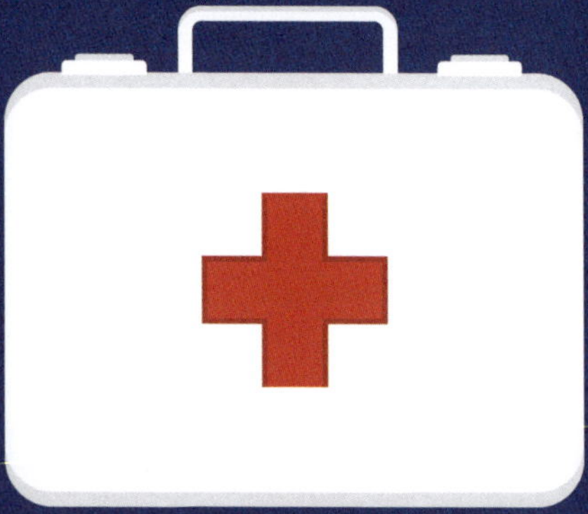

In facing the upstart Michael Jordan and the Chicago Bulls during their reign, the Bad Boys developed what were known as the "Jordan Rules," which amounted to clobbering Jordan every time he drove the ball to the hoop.

—

Reserve forward Vinnie Johnson was known as "the Microwave" for coming off the bench and instantly heating up the Pistons offense.

—

Forward Bill Laimbeer remains one of the most hated players in NBA history, despised by nearly every fan base outside of Detroit for his aggressive defensive tactics and surly attitude toward opponents and crowds.

National Basketball Association

"THE BAD BOYS"

The Detroit Pistons, late 1980's–early 1990's

In the "Bad Boys" era of the Detroit Pistons, the team, led by point guard Isiah Thomas, played tough, take-no-prisoners ball. Hard fouls and playing after the whistle were the rule, not the exception, which led to countless fights, technical fouls, and ejections for both the Pistons and their opponents. But their tactics worked. After a heartbreaking loss to the Boston Celtics in the 1988 Eastern Conference Finals, the Pistons won back-to-back championships, defeating the Los Angeles Lakers in 1989 and the Portland Trail Blazers in 1990.

> *You can say what you want about me, but you can't say that I'm not a winner.*
>
> —Isiah Thomas

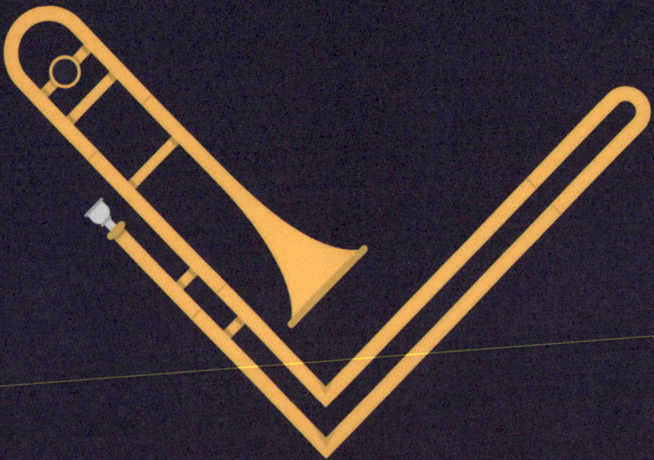

"The Play" consistently ranks as one of the best college football plays of all time.

—

Days after the game, Stanford students printed and distributed a fake version of the Cal student newspaper claiming the NCAA had declared the return illegal and gave the victory to Stanford.

College Football

"THE PLAY"

California vs. Stanford, 1982

Simply known as "The Play," the final seconds of the 1982 matchup between the University of California and Stanford was one of the craziest endings in the history of football. After being led down the field by quarterback John Elway, Stanford kicked a 35-yard field goal late in the fourth quarter to take the lead, 20–19. With eight seconds remaining and the game seemingly over, both teams lined up for the ensuing kickoff, and Stanford's kicker squibbed the ball to Cal's 46-yard line. Cal's Kevin Moen fielded the ball and headed toward the sideline, where he was met by a slew of Stanford defenders and so lateraled the ball to another Cal player before he was tackled. His teammates followed his lead, and laterals continued between several Cal players, who somehow eluded the pursuing Stanford defense while moving the ball toward the end zone. Thinking the game was over, Stanford's band began to play and made its way onto the field, unaware that play was still going on. Moen ended up with the ball again around Stanford's 25-yard line and ran it into the end zone in the midst of the band as time expired. He trampled a Stanford trombone player in the process. After the chaos settled, the officials gathered and decided Cal had won 25–20, despite protests and controversy regarding the play's legality.

> *Oh, the band is out on the field!*
> —Cal radio announcer Joe Starkey

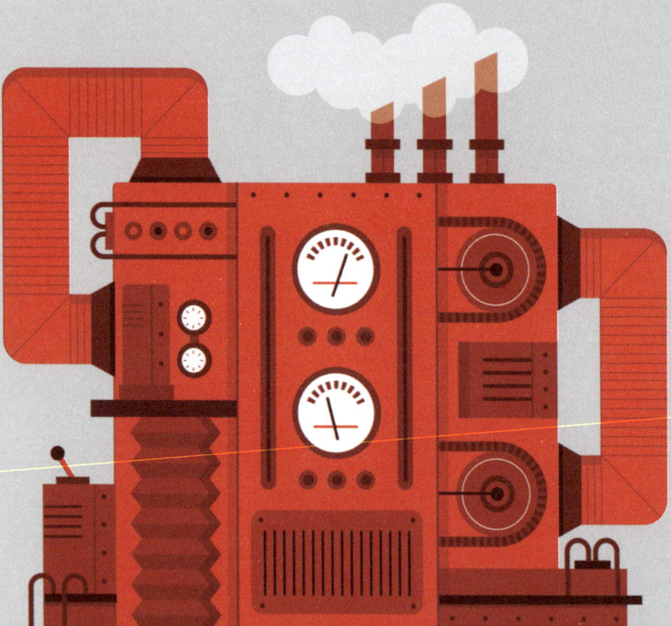

Major League Baseball

"THE BIG RED MACHINE"

Cincinnati Reds, 1970–76

"The Big Red Machine" was particularly punishing against the state of Pennsylvania, beating the Pittsburgh Pirates for their first three pennants, and the Philadelphia Phillies for their fourth.

—

In 1976 the Reds were offensively dominant, leading the National League in runs, hits, home runs, RBIs, and steals, en route to 102 wins.

—

Left fielder George Foster earned the nickname "the Destroyer" as one of the most feared power hitters of the era.

For six years in the 1970's, baseball was dominated by the Cincinnati Reds. Between 1970 and 1976 they won five division titles, four National League pennants, and two consecutive World Series championships. To fans, "The Big Red Machine" was the embodiment of what a baseball team should be: a fully functional collection of players who used their skills in tandem to create something magical on the field, bolstered by camaraderie and professionalism. Managed by Sparky Anderson, they fielded perhaps the greatest collection of position players in the history of baseball. Nicknamed the "Great Eight," the Reds lineup featured Hall of Famers Johnny Bench, Joe Morgan, and Tony Perez, along with all-time hits leader Pete Rose. Top to bottom, the Reds were a force to be reckoned with, winning games at a near .630 clip at their peak. When the Great Eight played together (nearly 100 games) during the 1975 and 1976 campaigns, their winning percentage increased to an absurd .784, unheard of for a team over that long a time period.

> *We didn't think we could get beat because we almost never did get beat.*
>
> —Joe Morgan, Cincinnati Reds second baseman, 1972–79

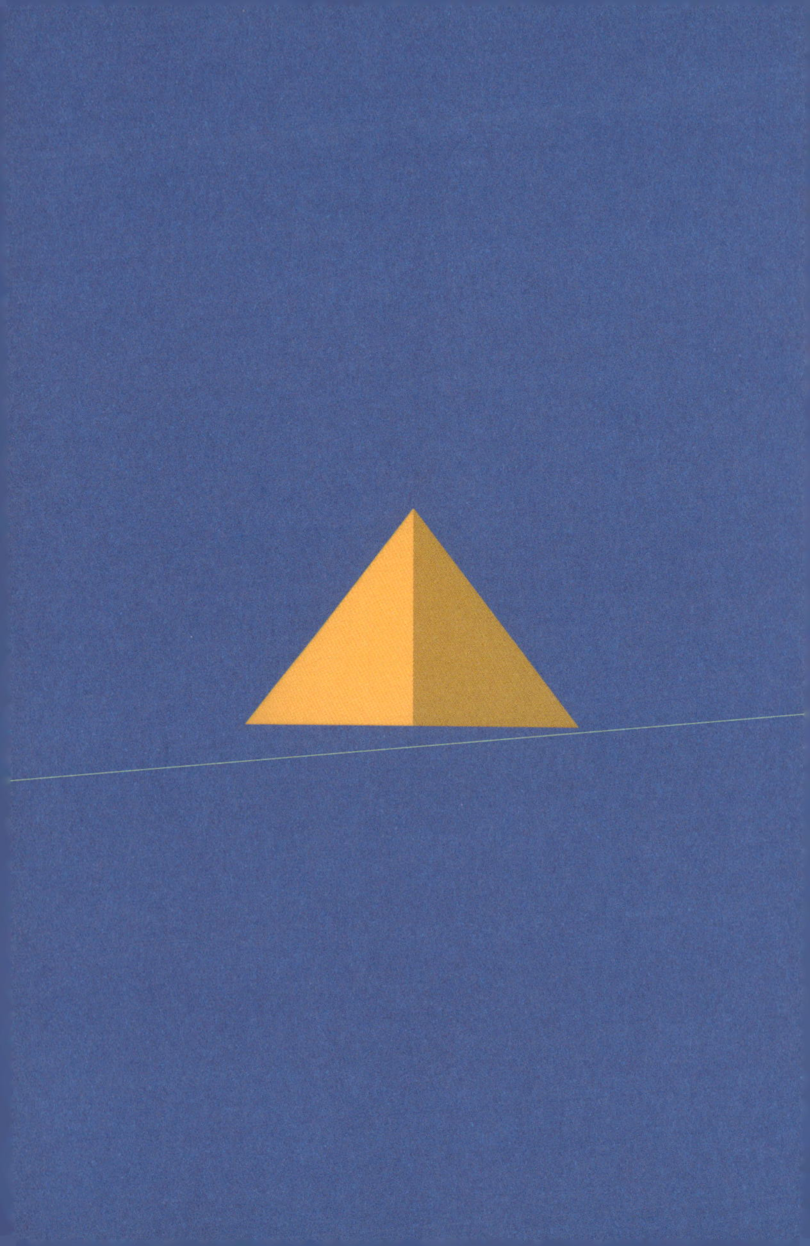

College Basketball

JOHN WOODEN
"The Wizard of Westwood"

Wooden's all-time coaching record was an astounding 664–162, winning more than 80 percent of his games.

—

Wooden was inducted into the Naismith Memorial Basketball Hall of Fame as a player in 1960 and as a coach in 1973.

—

Wooden was awarded the Presidential Medal of Freedom in 2003, the highest honor an American civilian can receive.

John Wooden's name and legacy are synonymous with the UCLA Bruins. One of the most successful coaches in any sport, Wooden took over as UCLA's head basketball coach in 1948 and turned a virtual nonentity in college basketball into a legendary team. Wooden implemented his "Pyramid of Success," a concept he developed to teach his players to rely on one another as well as themselves. He led the Bruins to back-to-back national championships in 1964 and 1965, and followed them up with the most commanding run in the history of college basketball. Beginning in 1967, Wooden coached the Bruins to seven straight national titles, anchored by dominant centers Lew Alcindor (later Kareem Abdul-Jabbar) and Bill Walton. The stretch also included an eighty-eight-game winning streak, and four undefeated seasons. Upon his retirement in 1975, Wooden had won a record ten national championships during his twenty-nine-year career.

> *Winning takes talent. To repeat takes character.*
> —John Wooden

National Football League

WILLIAM PERRY
"The Fridge"

With a size 25 finger, Perry holds the distinction of having the largest Super Bowl ring in history.

—

Perry won a National Championship at the University of Clemson in 1981, also earning All-American honors in 1983.

—

Perry's career offensive numbers included 8 carries for 5 yards, with 2 touchdowns.

Anchoring the Chicago Bears defensive line for most of the 1980's and early 1990's, William "The Refrigerator" Perry was one of the league's most recognizable and popular players. A massive individual, "The Fridge" used his 350-plus-pound frame to terrorize opposing quarterbacks and buffet lines, but became best known for his role in the Bears' offense. Drafted out of the University of Clemson in 1984, Perry quickly found himself at the center of a spat between Bears head coach Mike Ditka and defensive coordinator Buddy Ryan. Perry was a favorite of Ditka's before the draft, much to the chagrin of Ryan, who thought Ditka had wasted the pick. As Ryan refused to play Perry consistently, Ditka began inserting him into the game on offense, playing him at fullback near the goal line and other short-yardage situations, culminating with Perry scoring a one-yard touchdown during the Bears' victory in Super Bowl XX.

> *Even when I was little, I was big.*
> —William Perry

Acknowledgments

Thank you first and foremost to my mom and dad, for always encouraging me to draw and pursue my artistic endeavors.
To Melissa for playing catch with your little brother even when you didn't want to. To Aunt Marilyn for taking me to Lions games when I was growing up (except that one on Christmas Eve).
To Bill, Gar, Loren, Ryan, Mike, Muns, and all my friends for watching countless games with me.
To Mickey for encouraging me to start this whole thing.
To my editor, Jay Sacher, designers Danielle Deschenes and Ian Dingman, and the rest of the wondrous team at Clarkson Potter for turning this mess of ideas into a coherent book.
I couldn't have done it without all of you and am forever grateful.

INDEX

Ali, Muhammad (Cassius Clay), 17, 39, 61
American Basketball Association (ABA), 69
Anderson, Sparky, 41, 103
Auerbach, Red, 33
Auriemma, Geno, 45, 77

baseball, Major League
   Big Red Machine, 103
   Buckner's error, 25
   Cobb, Ty "Spikes Up," 73
   Fisk, Carlton, 41
   Jackson, Randy, 81
   Jackson, Reggie, 81, 95
   Mendoza line, 55
   pine tar incident (Royals vs. Yankees), 65
   Ryan, Nolan, 81
   Schilling's bloody sock, 7
basketball, college
   "Fab Five," 93
   Knight, Bobby, 9
   "Phi Slama Jama," 23
   Summitt, Pat, 45
   undefeated UConn women (2008–2010), 77
   Wooden, John, 105
basketball, professional
   American Basketball Association (ABA), 69
   Auerbach, Red, 33
   "Bad Boys," 99
   breaking color barrier in, 33
   Russell, Bill, 33
   Stockton, John, 53
Bench, Johnny, 41, 103
Borg, Björn, 47
Boston Red Sox, 7, 25, 41
boxing
   Ali vs. Frazier ("Thrilla in Manila"), 61
   Clay vs. Liston, 17
   Duran vs. Leonard ("*No más*"), 83
   Foreman vs. Ali ("Rumble in the Jungle"), 39
   Hearns vs. Hagler ("The War"), 97
Brett, George, 55, 65
Bryant, Paul W. "Bear," 19
Buckner, Bill, 25

Charles, Tina, 77

Chastain, Brandi, 57
Cincinnati Reds, 41, 103
Clark, Bobby, 59
Clay, Cassius, 17
Cobb, Ty "Spikes Up," 73
Comaneci, Nadia, 71
Connors, Jimmy, 13

Detroit Pistons "Bad Boys," 99
Drexler, Clyde, 23
Duran, Roberto, 83
Erving, Julius "Dr. J," 69

figure skating, 21
Fisk, Carlton, 41
Fleming, Peggy, 21
football, college
   Bryant, Paul W. "Bear," 19
   "Fifth Down" (Colorado vs. Missouri, 1990), 87
   "The Play" (California vs. Stanford, 1982), 101
football, NFL
   Davis, Al, 43
   Lott, Ronnie "9½ Fingers," 63
   Namath, Joe, 79
   Norwood, Scott, field goal miss, 91
   Perry, William "The Fridge," 107
   Sanders, Barry, 11
   Steel Curtain, 31
Foreman vs. Ali ("Rumble in the Jungle"), 39
Foster, George, 103
Frazier, Joe, 39, 61

Gervin, George, 69
Graf, Steffi, 29
Greene, "Mean Joe," 31
Greenwood, L. C., 31
gymnastics
   Comaneci, Nadia, 71
   Strug, Kerri, 85

Hagler, Marvin, 97
Hawkins, Connie, 69
Hearns, Thomas, 97
hockey, NHL
   Broad Street Bullies (Philadelphia Flyers), 59
   first goalie mask, 75
   Orr, Bobby, 15
   Plante, Jacques, 75
   Richard, Maurice "Rocket," 49
   Yzerman, Steve, 37

Holmes, Ernie, 31
Howard, Juwan, 93

Jackson, Ray, 93
Jackson, Reggie, 81, 95
Johnson, Charles, 87
Johnson, Randy, 81
Johnson, Vinnie, 99
Jordan, Michael, 99
Joyner, Florence Griffith "Flo Jo," 35, 51

Karolyi, Bela, 71, 85
Kelly, Bob "Hound Dog," 59
King, Billie Jean, 89
King, Jimmy, 93
Knight, Bobby, 9
Knoll, Chuck, 31

Laimbeer, Bill, 99
Leonard, Sugar Ray, 83
Lewis, Guy, 23
Liston, Sonny, 17
Lott, Ronnie "9½ Fingers," 63

Malone, Karl, 53
Maradona, Diego, 27
McEnroe, John, 13, 47
Mendoza line (Mario Mendoza), 55
Michaels, Al, 91, 97
Moore, Maya, 77
Morgan, Joe, 41, 103

Namath, Joe, 79
New York Jets, 79
New York Yankees, 7, 65, 95
Norwood, Scott, 91

Olajuwon, Hakeem, 23
Olympics
   basketball, 53
   boxing, 17, 83
   Chastain, Brandi, and, 57
   Clay, Cassius, and, 17
   Comaneci, Nadia, and, 71
   Duran, Roberto, and, 83
   figure skating team tragedy, 21
   Fleming, Peggy, and, 21
   Graf, Steffi, and, 29
   gymnastics, 71, 85
   Joyner, Florence Griffith "Flo Jo," and, 35, 51
   Leonard, Sugar Ray, and, 83
   Rudolph, Wilma "Skeeter," and, 51
   soccer, 57
   Stockton and Malone and, 53

Strug, Kerri, and, 85
   tennis, 29
   track and field, 35, 51
Orr, Bobby, 15

Perez, Tony, 41, 103
Perry, William "The Fridge," 107
Philadelphia Flyers (Broad Street Bullies), 59
Pittsburgh's Steel Curtain, 31
Plante, Jacques, 75

Richard, Maurice "Rocket," 49
Riggs, Bobby, 89
Rose, Jalen, 93
Rose, Pete, 103
Rudolph, Wilma "Skeeter," 51
Russell, Bill, 33
Ryan, Nolan, 81

Sanders, Barry, 11
Schilling, Curt, 7
Schultz, Dave "The Hammer," 59
Scurry, Briana, 57
soccer
   Chastain, Brandi, 57
   Maradona's "hand of God" goal, 27
   Women's World Cup (1999), 57
Stockton, John, 53
Strug, Kerri, 85
Summitt, Pat, 45

tennis
   "Battle of the Sexes" (King vs. Riggs), 89
   Borg's Grand Slam titles, 47
   Connors, Jimmy, 13
   Graf's Grand Slam titles, 29
   "Superbrat" McEnroe, 13, 47
   US Open Final (2001), 67
   Williams sisters, 67
Thomas, Isiah, 99
track and field
   Joyner, Florence Griffith "Flo Jo," 35, 51
   Rudolph, Wilma "Skeeter," 51

Webber, Chris, 93
White, Dwight, 31
Williams sisters (Venus vs. Serena), 67
Wooden, John, 105

Yzerman, Steve, 37

OZA LINE STEVE YZERM
FISK "THE PLAY" BRAND
CASSIUS CLAY VS. SO
BARRY SANDERS PEGGY
LLING DOC ELLIS "THE B
KERRI STRUG "THE BAT
OLAN RYAN SCOTT NOR
I "THE RUMBLE IN THE J
ARD BOBBY KNIGHT RE
AMA" DIEGO MARADONA
MERICAN BASKETBALL A
" NADIA COMANECI WI
WOMEN'S BASKETB

PAUL W. BRYANT
CHASTAIN BOBBY ORR
Y LISTON "THE BAD BOYS
EMING BILL BUCKNER
AD STREET BULLIES" ST
E OF THE SEXES" RONNI
OD ARNOLD JACOB AU
GLE" JACQUES PLANTE
E JACKSON "THE THRIL
HE BIG RED MACHINE" T
SOCIATION (ABA) "THE PI
A RUDOLPH FLORENCE G
HE FIFTH DOWN" 2001

GHS

If you enjoyed this book
or it has touched your life in some way,
we'd love to hear from you.

Please write a review at Hallmark.com,

e-mail us at booknotes@hallmark.com,

or send your comments to:

Hallmark Book Feedback

P.O. Box 419034

Mail Drop 100

Kansas City, MO 64141

"The Pine Tar Incident"
1983

John Stockton drafted by the Utah Jazz
1984

Hearns vs. Hagler
1985

Bill Buckner's fielding error, Game 6 of the World Series
1986

Ronnie Lott's left pinkie finger is amputated
1986

Bobby Knight coaches the Hoosiers to a third championship
1987

Florence Griffith Joyner wins three gold medals and a silver medal at the Seoul Olympics
1988

"The Fifth Down," University of Colorado vs. University of Missouri
1990